Sacraments and Justice

Sacraments and Justice

Edited by Doris Donnelly

A Michael Glazier Book

LITURGICAL PRESS
Collegeville, Minnesota

www.litpress.org

A Michael Glazier Book published by Liturgical Press

Cover design by Jodi Hendrickson. Cover image: Thinkstock.

1   2   3   4   5   6   7   8   9

Library of Congress Cataloging-in-Publication Data

Sacraments and justice / Doris K. Donnelly, editor.
    pages   cm
    ISBN 978-0-8146-8072-8 — ISBN 978-0-8146-8097-1 (ebook)
    1. Sacraments—Catholic Church.   2. Christianity and justice—Catholic Church.   I. Donnelly, Doris, editor.

BX2203.S24   2014
234'.16—dc23

2014020482

Contents

Introduction

There was a concern among theologians, liturgists, and church historians at the Second Vatican Council (1962–1965) that sacramental symbolism was not measuring up to its potential. In *Sacrosanctum Concilium* (the Constitution on the Sacred Liturgy),[1] the council urged that sacramental symbols be more transparent to their sacred reality and, implicitly, that whatever camouflaged transparency be either refreshed or eliminated so that mystery, and not confusion, could flourish.

It took a while for the revitalization process to take hold. Catholics, accustomed to an approach to sacraments that required little, if any, participation, were comfortable with passivity, and sometimes, sad to say, a "magical" understanding of sacraments. The liturgical renewal proposed at the Second Vatican Council, on the other hand, invited active participation, personal involvement, and commitment. The council understood sacramental symbols as actions, not objects.[2] That orientation encouraged beholding not bread, oil, and water, but participating in the powerful symbolism of *breaking bread* so that all might be fed, of *drowning* by immersion in baptismal waters as more closely revealing a death and rebirth in Christ than did drops of water on a person's forehead, of *burnishing* confirmands, the newly ordained, and the sick with oil for strength in what lay ahead, and of *hearing* and *trusting* words of mutual commitment spoken in marriage and of forgiveness spoken in penance as effecting what they signify.

---

[1] All quotations from the Second Vatican Council used in this volume are taken from *Vatican Council II: The Basic Sixteen Documents; Constitutions, Decrees, Declarations*, ed. Austin Flannery (Collegeville, MN: Liturgical Press, 2014).

[2] Nathan Mitchell, " 'Symbols are Actions, Not Objects'—New Directions for an Old Problem," in *Living Worship*, a publication of the Liturgical Conference, February 1977, 13:2.

Sacraments go beyond "representing" another reality. In a class of their own, sacramental symbols are intimately connected with the reality they express. Baffling to nonbelievers unable to decipher them, misrepresented by those who misread and often reduce symbols to mere signs, sacramental symbols are sources of joy, solace, confrontation, peace, healing, strength, and life-giving sustenance to the initiated.

As symbols were resuscitated and sacraments were renewed, each of the seven—baptism, confirmation, Eucharist, penance, marriage, orders, and the anointing of the sick—uncovered a link to social justice, understood in these pages as a call for harmony and well-being of all in society where there exists equality of chances in education and employment, appropriate living conditions, and access to health care.

Few understand that link better than the authors represented in these pages.

Each writer is a theologian with pastoral sensitivities. Some are married, some are parents, some are pastors, and some are priests. All are educators aware of the social implications of worship, able to communicate not only the history of each sacrament but also the active presence of Christ who lives in expectation that each of us will participate in the urgent renewal of unjust policies and systems that affect the most vulnerable in our global family.

The privilege of working with my colleagues on *Sacraments and Justice* was made possible by a Grauel Fellowship with the unfailing support of the former dean and now provost at JCU, Jeanne Colleran, and from Reverend Robert L. Niehoff, SJ, who, in addition to his responsibilities as president of John Carroll University, happens also to be a naturally gifted liturgist and homilist.

Editing this volume has been a labor of love.

Doris Donnelly
May 11, 2014

1

Baptism and Justice

John F. Baldovin, SJ

Near the end of Francis Ford Coppola's first *Godfather* film, Michael, the youngest Corleone son, has been forced by circumstances to take charge of the "family business"—organized crime. His father has died a natural death, but his older brother, Sonny, has been murdered by a rival crime family. Michael plots revenge, and in a frighteningly vivid scene we witness the baptism of his sister's child interspersed with scenes of the murder of Michael's enemies, murders committed on Michael's orders. Michael, as the new godfather, even plans to have his brother-in-law, the father of the baptized child, murdered immediately after the baptism for his betrayal of the family and the part he played in Sonny's death. Michael's facial expression as he answers the baptismal questions about renunciation of evil and profession of faith is telling. One senses his recognition of the utter hypocrisy of his actions.

Sometimes it takes a counterexample to heighten our own awareness of the meaning of a sacramental act. The contradiction here is quite clear—one cannot at one and the same time affirm the life that is given to the children of God and commit murder.

Baptism Today

> Baptism is participation in Christ's death and resurrection (Rom
> 6:3-5; Col 2:12); a washing away of sin (1 Cor 6:11); a new birth (John
> 3:5); an enlightenment by Christ (Eph 5:14); a re-clothing in Christ
> (Gal 3:27); a renewal by the Spirit (Tit 3:5); the experience of salvation
> from the flood (1 Pet 3:20-21); an exodus from bondage (1 Cor 10:1-2)
> and a liberation into a new humanity in which barriers of division
> whether of sex or race or social status are transcended. (Gal 3:27-28;
> 1 Cor 12:13).[1]

The landmark ecumenical convergence document *Baptism, Eucharist, and Ministry* (BEM) contains a number of essential affirmations about the Christian life. It is a fine starting point for understanding baptism today. Baptism is the formal beginning of the Christian life and (at least in adults and children of catechetical age) the culmination of a process of conversion to Christ. (I was tempted to write "conclusion to the process," but of course the Christian life is one of constant and deeper conversion.)

In the New Testament Jesus is himself baptized by John the Baptist (Mark 1:9-11; Matt 3:13-17; Luke 3:21-22).[2] Jesus associates baptism with his death in Mark 10:38-40. Baptism is clearly indicated as the means of formal entry into Christian living in the Acts of the Apostles (Acts 1:5-6, 2:37-42, 8:26-30, 10:44-48). John's gospel spells out the necessity of baptism as being "born from above" in the dialogue with Nicodemus (John 3:1-21). Finally, in exhorting his correspondents to live a truly Christian life, Paul reminds them that their baptism was a participation in Christ's death and burial (Rom 6:3-11). There are, then, a variety of metaphors used for baptism in the New Testament: new birth, enlightenment, and cleansing, as well as death and resurrection.

In the early church, for the most part, adults were initiated in the sequence: baptism, chrismation (or imposition of hands), and first

---

[1] Faith and Order Commission (World Council of Churches), "Baptism," in *Baptism, Eucharist, and Ministry, Faith and Order Paper 111* (Geneva: 1982), 1, para. 2.

[2] On this and many other issues treated in this essay, see Maxwell Johnson, *The Rites of Christian Initiation*, rev. ed. (Collegeville, MN: Liturgical Press, 2007). See also E. C. Whitaker, *Documents of the Baptismal Liturgy*, 3rd ed. (London: SPCK, 2003).

Eucharist.[3] In the course of the rites they exchanged the kiss of peace for the first time and joined in the prayers of the faithful. Their preparation included a period of instruction, training, and exorcisms that could last up to three years.[4] A final period of the catechumenate, as it was known, began with the enrollment of names at the beginning of Lent, the reception of the Creed and the Lord's Prayer, and a final series of exorcisms, called the scrutinies.[5] The catechumens, at this point called "the Elect," were baptized, were chrismated, and received the Eucharist during the course of the great vigil of Easter on Holy Saturday night. As newborn Christians (neophytes) they were then instructed on the rites in which they had participated, the so-called period of mystagogy. The mass conversion to Christianity encouraged the widespread practice of infant baptism, which itself inspired St. Augustine of Hippo to argue for the universality of original sin.[6]

In the course of the Middle Ages, Eastern and Western Christianity divided in their approach to baptismal practice. The Christian East retained the integrity of initiation as well as the traditional sequence of baptism-chrismation-Eucharist. The principle of ecclesial unity, always important for initiation, was signified by the fact that only a bishop was able to consecrate chrism, the oil used in the postbaptismal anointing.[7] In the West, however, unity was signified by the person of the bishop himself. Eventually, when infants were baptized by presbyters, their baptism was confirmed (completed) by the imposition of hands and anointing by the bishop. In this way, confirmation was sundered from the original integrity of the initiatory scheme. Many churches retained the original sequence (baptism-chrismation-Eucharist), but in the course of time, first Eucharist began to precede

---

[3] "For the most part," since there were regions like Syria where the sequence seems to have been Anointing-Baptism-Eucharist. See Johnson, *Rites of Christian Initiation*, 55–63.

[4] At least according to *The Apostolic Tradition*, see Whitaker, *Documents of the Baptismal Liturgy*.

[5] Once again, I am painting with a broad brush and homogenizing practices from a number of geographical areas and across centuries. We only know of the official enrollment of names, for example, from the late fourth century on.

[6] See Everett Ferguson, *Baptism in the Early Church* (Grand Rapids, MI: Eerdmans, 2009), 804ff.

[7] See Johnson, *Rites*, 275–307.

confirmation, especially when confirmation began to be given in adolescence.

One of the major achievements of the Second Vatican Council's document *Sacrosanctum Concilium* (the Constitution on the Sacred Liturgy) was the restoration of the catechumenate for adults and the creation of an explicit rite geared to the baptism of children.[8] Here is what the Constitution has to say:

> 64. The catechumenate for adults, divided into several distinct steps, is to be restored and brought into use at the discretion of the local Ordinary. By this means, the time of the catechumenate, which is destined for the requisite formation, may be sanctified by sacred rites to be celebrated at successive stages.
>
> 65. In mission countries, in addition to what is found in the christian tradition, those elements of initiation may be admitted which are already in use among every people, insofar as they can be adapted to the Christian ritual in accordance with articles 37-40 of this constitution.
>
> 66. Both rites for the Baptism of adults are to be revised, not only the simpler rite but also, taking into consideration the restored cate-chumenate, the more solemn rite. A special Mass "For the conferring of Baptism" is to be inserted into the Roman Missal.
>
> 67. The rite for the Baptism of infants is to be revised. The revision should take into account the fact that those to be baptized are babies. The roles of parents and godparents, and also their duties, should be brought out more clearly in the rite itself.
>
> 68. The baptismal rite should contain variants, to be used at the discretion of the local Ordinary, when a large number is to be baptized. Likewise a shorter rite is to be drawn up, especially for mission countries, which may be used by catechists when neither priest nor deacon is available and, when there is danger of death, by the faithful in general.
>
> 69. In place of what is known as the "Rite for making up for what was omitted in the Baptism of an infant" a new rite is to be drawn up. This rite should indicate more fittingly and clearly that the infant baptized by the short rite has already been received into the church.

---

[8] For centuries the rite of baptism for infants was simply an abbreviated form of the rite for adults suitable for emergencies, hence "clinical" baptism; see Mark Searle, *Christening: The Making of Christians* (Collegeville, MN: Liturgical Press, 1980).

Thus the council was responsible for the Rite of Baptism of Infants, issued in 1968, and the Rite of Christian Initiation of Adults, issued in 1972. Although many thought that a restored catechumenate would be employed mainly in "mission lands," it quickly became clear that it was to provide a model for what it means to belong to the church—everywhere.[9]

Two further comments are appropriate with regard to what *Sacrosanctum Concilium* tried to achieve with initiation. First, note that the constitution's section on cultural adaptation in 37–40 is specifically mentioned. It was later understood that cultural adaptation (or inculturation, as it came to be called) was necessary everywhere. In addition, there is a new concern for the adaptation of the rites to particular circumstances, e.g., those of the infant. The rites for adults and for infants that were produced subsequent to Vatican II took these guidelines into consideration. There are a number of places in the Rite of Christian Initiation of Adults, for example, where a good deal of latitude in ritual action and wording is allowed. In infant baptism, the godparents no longer act as "liturgical ventriloquists" mouthing the renunciations and faith of the child. Now the faith of the church is explicitly professed by the parents and godparents as their own faith.

Finally, we should note the widespread practice of baptizing infants at parish eucharistic celebrations on Sundays. The connection between baptism and the church is made much more explicit by this practice.

At this point, it should be obvious that baptism is much more than cleansing from sin—original in the case of infants, and of all sin in the case of adults. Baptism, as the BEM document points out, is also participation in Christ's death and resurrection, entrance into the body of Christ, the church, liberation from bondage, and renewal in the Spirit.

Among the motifs spelled out in BEM is a concern for the ethical character of the Christian life: "a liberation into a new humanity in

[9] See the excellent commentary by Aidan Kavanagh, *The Shape of Baptism: The Rite of Christian Initiation*, rev. ed. (Collegeville, MN: Liturgical Press, 1991).

which barriers of division whether of sex or race or social status are transcended (Gal 3:27-28; 1 Cor 12:13)."[10]

Ethical concerns appear with some frequency in the document's section on the Eucharist, in particular with regard to the communion of the faithful and the meal of the kingdom, both of which demand that the Eucharist itself mirror a just society. They appear as well in the passage cited above that includes the vision of a new humanity in which the usual boundaries that bring about injustice are dissolved. Liberation from these barriers is listed among the meanings of baptism.

The remainder of this chapter is an attempt to unfold the meaning of baptism (Christian initiation in general) as an effective sign of social justice. Clearly one of the essential tasks for Christian theology today is to explain the profound connections between the celebration of the sacraments and Christian life in general. My thesis here is the same as Robert Taft's, when he says "the liturgy is Christian life in a nutshell."[11] Somehow, fifty years after Vatican II's Constitution on the Sacred Liturgy, this connection between liturgy and life has become lost on the majority of Christians. Perhaps this essay as well as others in this collection may be a small step in ameliorating that misunderstanding.

Baptism and Justice in the New Testament

The writings of the New Testament provide a number of clear indications of the human dignity that comes with Christian baptism. The first letter of Peter is considered by a number of commentators as a baptismal homily. The nobility of the Christian calling and the fundamental equality of the baptized is suggested by 1 Peter 2:9-10:

> But you are a chosen race, a royal priesthood, a holy nation, God's own people, in order that you may proclaim the mighty acts of him who called you out of darkness into his marvelous light.
> Once you were not a people,
> but now you are God's people;

---

[10] Faith and Order Commission, *Baptism, Eucharist, and Ministry.*

[11] Robert Taft, *The Liturgy of the Hours in East and West*, 2nd ed. (Collegeville, MN: Liturgical Press, 1993), 340–46.

once you had not received mercy,
but now you have received mercy.

If it really is the case that baptized Christians constitute a chosen race, a royal priesthood, and a holy nation, then any form of injustice within the Christian family is unthinkable.

Similarly, in reminding his correspondents that all are baptized in the Spirit into one body (1 Cor 12:4-13), Paul makes it quite clear that all are dependent on one another. All the baptized are intimately inter-related, just as a body only works if all its parts are coordinated:

> Now there are varieties of gifts, but the same Spirit; and there are varieties of services, but the same Lord; and there are varieties of activities, but it is the same God who activates all of them in every-one. To each is given the manifestation of the Spirit for the common good. To one is given through the Spirit the utterance of wisdom, and to another the utterance of knowledge according to the same Spirit, to another faith by the same Spirit, to another gifts of healing by the one Spirit, to another the working of miracles, to another prophecy, to another the discernment of spirits, to another various kinds of tongues, to another the interpretation of tongues. All these are activated by one and the same Spirit, who allots to each one individually just as the Spirit chooses.
>
> For just as the body is one and has many members, and all the members of the body, though many, are one body, so it is with Christ. For in the one Spirit we were all baptized into one body—Jews or Greeks, slaves or free—and we were all made to drink of one Spirit.

Finally, in making his case to the Galatians with regard to the new relationship that Christians have to the Mosaic Law, Paul delivers a memorable and powerful message about the radical equality of the baptized:

> As many of you as were baptized into Christ have clothed yourselves with Christ. There is no longer Jew or Greek, there is no longer slave or free, there is no longer male and female; for all of you are one in Christ Jesus. (Gal 3:27-28)

Given modern sensitivities about social justice, many today have pointed to Galatians 3:27-28 as a charter statement against all forms of discrimination within the church.

The Early Church

Augustine and the Fundamental Equality of the Baptized

Some have argued that the primary sacrament in the early church was baptism. Perhaps more accurately, one can say that the initiatory sequence—baptism, chrismation, Eucharist—constituted the central sacramental imagination and practice of Christians. A number of early Christian writers testify to the importance and dignity of the baptismal state, among them Cyril of Jerusalem, Ambrose of Milan, and John Chrysostom.[12] But perhaps no one preaches so elegantly on the topic as St. Augustine of Hippo.[13] The following is an excerpt from his (justly) famous Easter sermon to the newly baptized in Hippo, given on the last day of Pentecost and dated to the second decade of the fifth century:

> If you desire to understand the Body of Christ, listen to the apostle who tells the faithful, "Now you are the Body of Christ and its members" [1 Cor 12:27]. If, therefore, you are the Body and the members of Christ, your mystery is placed on the Lord's table; you receive your own mystery. Respond "Amen" to what you are, and by responding you give your assent. You hear "The Body of Christ" and you respond "Amen." Be a member of Christ's Body so that your Amen may be true. Why in bread? So that we may bring nothing of our own here, let us listen to the same apostle who says about this sacrament, "We though many are one bread, one body" [1 Cor 10:17]. Understand and rejoice: unity, truth, godliness, love. "One bread." Who is this one bread? "Many are one body." Further reflect on the fact that the bread is made from many grains, not from one grain. When you were exorcised, you were, so to speak, ground in a mill. When you were baptized, you were, so to speak, mixed together like dough. When you received the fire of the Holy Spirit, you were, so to speak, baked. Be what you can see, and receive what you are.[14]

[12] See Edward Yarnold, *The Awe-Inspiring Rites of Initiation*, 2nd ed. (Collegeville, MN: Liturgical Press, 1994).

[13] For a comprehensive study of initiation in early Christianity, specifically with regard to Augustine, see Ferguson, *Baptism in the Early Church*, 776–816.

[14] See Lawrence Johnson, *Worship in the Early Church*, vol. 3 (Collegeville, MN: Liturgical Press, 2009), 77. See also the recent study by Garry Wills, *Font of Life: Ambrose, Augustine, and the Mystery of Baptism* (New York: Oxford University Press, 2012).

Baptism and Justice 9

Augustine here underlines the corporate unity of Christians who receive the Eucharist by means of a description of the process of initiation. Just as bread is produced by a process that involves grinding, moistening, and baking, so Christians are formed into one body in Christ. This is a fine example of how our fundamental unity, equality, and interdependence is mirrored in our sacramental life.

Chrysostom on the Dignity of Baptism

John Chrysostom, presbyter at Antioch and later archbishop of Constantinople, delivered a number of baptismal catecheses. The following passage helps us to understand his justified reputation for eloquence:

> 5. "Blessed be God," we repeat it, "for he has done wonderful things," he who makes and renews all things. Those who yesterday were captives are today free, being citizens of the Church. Those who recently were in the shame of sin are now assured of justice. They are not only free, but also holy; not only holy, but just; not only just, but children; not only children, but inheritors; not only inheritors, but brothers [and sisters] of Christ; not only brothers [and sisters] of Christ, but also his joint heirs; not only his joint heirs, but his members; not only his members, but also the temple; not only the temple, but also instruments of the Spirit.
>
> 6. "Blessed be God who alone does wonderful things." You have seen how numerous are the benefits of baptism. Although many believe that its only benefit is the remission of sins, we have counted ten honors that are conferred by it. This is why we baptize small infants even though they are sinless. We do so that they may be given justice, filial adoption, inheritance, that they may become brothers [and sisters] and members of Christ and may become the dwelling place of the Holy Spirit.[15]

In addition to being rhetorically impressive, this passage illuminates the dignity of Christian baptism—well beyond the forgiveness

---

[15] See Lawrence Johnson, *Worship in the Early Church*, vol. 2 (Collegeville, MN: Liturgical Press, 2009), 201–2.

of sin.[16] Baptism demands a treatment of others that recognizes them as heirs of Christ and temples of the Holy Spirit.

BEM and the Ethical Implications of Baptism

As we saw earlier in this chapter, the BEM document devotes considerable attention to the ethical implications of baptism, Eucharist, and ministry. The ethical dimensions of baptism are suggested in the document's attempt to emphasize its ecumenical dimension:

> D. Incorporation into the Body of Christ
>
> 6. Administered in obedience to our Lord, baptism is a sign and seal of our common discipleship. Through baptism, Christians are brought into union with Christ, with each other and with the Church of every time and place. Our common baptism, which unites us to Christ in faith, is thus a basic bond of unity. We are one people and are called to confess and serve one Lord in each place and in all the world. The union with Christ which we share through baptism has important implications for Christian unity. "There is . . . one baptism, one God and Father of all . . ." (Eph 4:4-6). When baptismal unity is realized in one holy, catholic, apostolic Church, a genuine Christian witness can be made to the healing and reconciling love of God. Therefore, our one baptism into Christ constitutes a call to the churches to overcome their divisions and visibly manifest their fellowship.[17]

The ecumenical movement has helped to foster the conviction that what unites us in baptism is deeper than what may divide us in terms of the churches to which we belong. I would add that this kind of respect is essential to an attitude of doing social justice that is even wider than the worldwide fellowship of Christians. The document's section on the Eucharist goes even further in spelling out the justice implications of Christian baptism:

> Since the earliest days, baptism has been understood as the sacrament by which believers are incorporated into the body of Christ and are endowed with the Holy Spirit. As long as the right of the

---

[16] Note that original sin does not seem to be an issue for Chrysostom, since he mentions that infants are baptized regardless of being sinless.

[17] Faith and Order Commission, "Eucharist as Communion of the Faithful," in *Baptism, Eucharist, and Ministry,* 12, para. 19.

baptized believers and their ministers to participate in and preside over Eucharistic celebration in one church is called into question by those who preside over and are members of other Eucharistic congregations, the catholicity of the Eucharist is less manifest. There is discussion in many churches today about the inclusion of baptized children as communicants at the Lord's Supper.[18]

On the basis of what one could call a baptismal ecclesiology, the BEM document challenges churches to examine themselves with regard to their own practice of justice.

Baptism and Its Implications

In their book, *The Liturgy That Does Justice*, James Empereur and Christopher Kiesling approach the subject of Christian initiation from the angle of the liberation of Israel from bondage in Egypt. They adopt the Vatican II (and of course, the biblical) image of the people of God as their lens. This enables them to link the liberation won by Jesus with a liberation from unjust social structures.[19] One can find a similar implication in the sacrifice of the first fruits in Deuteronomy 26. After the harvest, the people are instructed to bring their first fruits to the priests who will offer them to God. At the same time, the people recite God's marvelous deeds in rescuing them ("us") from Egypt. The passage does not end with the ritual sacrifice, however. It ends with the following:

> When you have finished paying all the tithe of your produce in the third year (which is the year of the tithe), giving it to the Levites, the aliens, the orphans, and the widows, so that they may eat their fill within your towns, then you shall say before the LORD your God: "I have removed the sacred portion from the house, and I have given it to the Levites, the resident aliens, the orphans, and the widows, in accordance with your entire commandment that you commanded me." (Deut 26:12-13)

In other words, having become a people liberated from slavery, the Israelites are now to recognize their justice obligations to the

---

[18] Ibid.

[19] See James Empereur and Christopher Kiesling, *The Liturgy That Does Justice* (Collegeville, MN: Liturgical Press, 1990), 41–48.

oppressed. Sacramental theologian Louis-Marie Chauvet calls this the process of symbolic exchange, whereby our liturgical actions are verified by how we live out what we have been given with our lives.[20]

Empereur and Kiesling also find a call to justice quite explicitly formulated in the American Episcopal *Book of Common Prayer* with its baptismal covenant:[21]

> Will you strive for justice and peace among all people,
> and respect the dignity of every human being?[22]

Here it is quite clear that receiving one's own baptismal dignity implies recognizing the dignity and human rights of all people. Similarly, William Reiser has suggested a reformulation of baptismal promises adapted to our contemporary circumstances, among them:

> Do you dedicate yourself to seeking the kingdom of God and God's justice, to praying daily, to meditating on the gospels and to celebrating the Eucharist faithfully and devoutly?
>
> Do you commit yourself to that simplicity of living which Jesus enjoined on his disciples? Do you commit yourself to resisting the spirit of materialism and consumerism which is so strong in our culture?
>
> Do you accept responsibility for building community, for being people of compassion and reconciliation, for being mindful of those who are poor and oppressed, and for truly forgiving those who have offended you?[23]

Reiser's contention is that we need a fresh look at our baptismal promises and the kind of evil that we are renouncing with such formulaic phrases as: "Do you renounce evil and refuse to be mastered by sin?" Often enough the antiquity of our formulas make it difficult to appreciate their modern applications.

---

[20] Louis-Marie Chauvet, *Symbol and Sacrament: A Sacramental Reinterpretation of Christian Existence*, ed. and trans. P. Madigan and M. Beaumont (Collegeville, MN: Liturgical Press, 1995), 231–39, 266ff.

[21] Empereur and Kiesling, *The Liturgy That Does Justice*, 49–50.

[22] *Book of Common Prayer* (New York: Church Publishing, 1979), 304–5.

[23] William Reiser, *Renewing the Baptismal Promises: Their Meaning for the Christian Life* (New York: Pueblo, 1988), 12–13.

Before the conversion of the emperor Constantine to Christianity in the fourth century, Christians had little difficulty appreciating the seriousness of their faith. They ran the risk of at least periodic persecutions for their baptismal commitment! The practical meaning of baptism then was a commitment to a way of life significantly transformed by the triumph of infant baptism and an overwhelming concern with original sin. It may be that the imbalance which that concern fostered has been mitigated today by the recovery of the adult catechumenate and the Rite of Christian Initiation of Adults. The challenge for the future is to help parents and families of those who are baptized in infancy to appreciate how momentous Christian baptism really is.

Returning to *The Godfather*

The violence of the concluding scenes of *The Godfather* reviewed at the opening of this chapter, with Michael Corleone flaunting un-Christian values in the murder of his enemies during the baptism of his nephew, offers a vivid example of how easily we can dissociate our liturgical and sacramental acts from the way we live our lives.

The film biography of Archbishop Oscar Romeo of San Salvador, *Romero*, serves as a countercultural response to the *Godfather*. It opens with a cleric, Romero, who has recently become archbishop and is friendly with the rich and important families that make up El Salvador's ruling oligarchy. But he is transformed by the assassination of a friend, the Jesuit Rutilio Grande, who has been preaching social justice. He experiences a conversion to Gospel justice for the poor and oppressed of his country. Shortly afterward, one of his rich friends comes and asks him to baptize her baby. He is delighted. She suggests a Sunday in December and he says, "Wonderful, that's a very popular time; there will be a lot of people coming to be baptized." She tells him they were hoping for a private baptism. "We don't do that," he responds. "You mean you want me to baptize my baby with a bunch of Indians?" He nods his head and she says, "You have deserted us." The incident sets the scene for the increasing opposition to Romero by the ruling oligarchy, but it also says something significant about baptism. In committing himself to social justice, the archbishop has realized that the sacramental sphere must mirror economic and social realities. To allow a private baptism simply because his friend cannot imagine mixing with "those Indians" would be a betrayal of a far different sort. It would be an outright contradiction to the meaning of Christian baptism itself.

The blindness of Archbishop Romero's rich friend to the fundamental equality and dignity of human beings is a chilling reminder of our need to recover a truly baptismal ecclesiology. That recovery can be part of a renewed appreciation of the rich life offered us in union with Christ—the life offered in Christian baptism.

2

Confirmation and Justice

Edward P. Hahnenberg

During college I volunteered on the campus ministry team for the Rite of Christian Initiation of Adults (RCIA) program. Each year we organized weekly classes, service days, retreats, and liturgies for a small group of students who wanted to become Catholic. It was always an amazing journey—one that culminated every spring at the Easter Vigil Mass celebrated in our campus chapel. Late that night, in a candle-lit church, surrounded by family and friends, the elect were baptized, confirmed, and received their first Communion. As the organ swelled and the choir chanted, these women and men began their Christian lives drenched in water, smeared with oil, and robed in white. They had tears in their eyes and smiles on their faces as the whole community embraced them with applause. It was an event both dramatic and intimate, charged with all the ancient power and mystery that first gave birth to these "awe-inspiring" rites of initiation.[1]

One year, a sophomore, whom we will call Dan, joined the program. Dan had been baptized as an infant, but had received no further

---

[1] Edward Yarnold, *The Awe-Inspiring Rites of Initiation: The Origins of the RCIA*, 2nd ed. (Collegeville, MN: Liturgical Press, 1993).

formation in the faith. He never made his first Communion. He had never been confirmed. As was our practice, the campus ministry team welcomed him into the RCIA program. Since he had already been baptized, he would be a "candidate," preparing for confirmation and Eucharist alongside the "catechumens" who were preparing for all three sacraments of initiation.

Dan was a nice guy, very likeable and very sincere. But he was rather absentminded and totally unreliable. He missed most of the sessions, often disappearing for weeks at a time, only to show up again out of the blue, as likeable and sincere as ever.

As Easter approached, we began to worry about Dan. Was this going to happen? Had Dan been adequately prepared? Was he taking it seriously? Would he even show up?

Our team leader, Tami, sent a letter to each member of the entire group with the schedule for Holy Week. It included a reminder to the candidates that they should receive the sacrament of reconciliation before the Easter Vigil. Still no word from Dan.

Then, Wednesday of Holy Week, Dan left a frantic message on Tami's voice mail: "Tami, I got your letter. I'm really hoping to do this on Saturday. But I haven't received the sacrament of reconciliation yet."

He continued, "I didn't get the sacrament. Maybe it got lost in the mail. Do you have an extra one? I could pick it up after class."

Faith in a Consumer Culture

When Tami shared Dan's message with the rest of the ministry team, we all laughed—not so much at Dan's innocence, but at our own failure at sacramental catechesis! It got me thinking about the kind of language we use to describe the sacraments. Who could blame Dan? After all, don't we often speak about the sacraments in ways that reduce them to *things* that we "get" or "receive"? In our consumer culture, is it possible that we even start to imagine the sacraments as *commodities* within some sacred economy of exchange?

In the end, Dan agreed to wait for his confirmation and first Communion. The following year he returned to the RCIA program, still clueless, but more committed. And I kept thinking about the way we imagine the sacraments. How does our participation in contemporary society affect our experience of the sacramental life? How does our participation in the sacramental life affect our experience of contemporary society? Understanding the relationship of sacraments to justice requires reflecting on the social and cultural context within which the quest for justice takes shape. Inspired by Dan's misunderstanding, I would like to focus on one particular dimension, namely, our existence within consumer culture.

In a complex and affluent nation like the United States, it is hard to find a dynamic that is more powerful or pervasive than consumerism. Long before we could speak, we were socialized into our roles, subtly trained to approach the world as a cornucopia of commodities. Over the course of our lives, this silent education continues. Every time we go to the grocery store or to the mall, we are taught to see things as disconnected from one another, independent and exchangeable. That is how commodities work. They are severed from their context in order to be put up for sale. Thus, we are divorced from the process by which commodities come to us. We do not see who harvested or made them, how they are brought to us, or what impact they have on the environment. Their only value lies in the price we are willing to pay to acquire them.

Consumption is not, in and of itself, an evil. After all, a certain amount of it is necessary for sustaining human life, which is a good. The trouble comes when the modern structures of consumption so fragment human life that they marginalize all other concerns. The market becomes the ultimate arbiter of value, and economics dictate *everything*. We elect leaders, launch wars, manipulate markets, and slowly destroy the very environment that sustains our life under an all-embracing banner promoting a single imperative: the freedom to consume. In the meantime, our consumer culture keeps us at a remove from all those who are left out or ground under by our desire for more. We fail to see the farmers, miners, textile workers, and all others on whose lives rest our own lives of easy consumption. "[T]he cultural situation in the United States, satiated by consumer goods and propelled by electronic technology," as Walter Brueggemann sharply put it, "is one of narcoticized insensibility to human reality."[2]

This manner of relating to material commodities pollutes the rest of our lives. We experience our daily labor, our homes, our relationships,

---

[2] Walter Brueggemann, *The Prophetic Imagination*, 2nd ed. (Minneapolis, MN: Fortress Press, 2001), xx.

our values, even our faith in economic, consumption-driven terms. When Dan asked how he could "get" another sacrament of reconciliation, he inadvertently reduced a relationship to a thing, a commodity. But he was only responding to the commodified way we so often talk about the sacraments. We treat elements of our faith as if they were products for exchange; thus, diluting them of their transforming power.[3]

Consumer culture offers up a vision of life radically different from the one proclaimed by Jesus of Nazareth. Jesus began his public ministry with the words of the prophet Isaiah:

> The Spirit of the Lord is upon me,
> because he has anointed me
> to bring good news to the poor.
> He has sent me to proclaim release to the captives
> and recovery of sight to the blind,
> to let the oppressed go free,
> to proclaim the year of the Lord's favor. (Luke 4:18-19)

According to Jesus, the anointing of the Spirit brings with it a call to peace, justice, and solidarity with those who suffer—in other words, it brings the reign of God. In Jesus' preaching of the reign of God, we find an alternative vision to the one offered by our present consumer culture. In the pages that follow, I will argue that the sacraments in general—and the sacrament of confirmation in particular—hold the potential to draw us into this alternative vision.

I will do so by highlighting three themes that have been associated with confirmation over the centuries: (1) the gift of the Spirit, (2) the church community, and (3) prophetic witness. The Second Vatican Council said little about confirmation and even less about the implications of this sacrament for justice. But *Lumen Gentium* (the Dogmatic Constitution on the Church) did offer this summary:

> By the sacrament of Confirmation [the faithful] are more perfectly bound to the church and are endowed with the special strength of the Holy Spirit. Hence, as true witnesses of Christ, they are more

---

[3] For an insightful treatment on the relation of consumer culture to faith, see Vincent J. Miller, *Consuming Religion: Christian Faith and Practice in a Consumer Culture* (New York: Continuum, 2004).

strictly obliged both to spread and to defend the faith by word and deed. (LG 11)[4]

In this brief passage, the council drew together the three themes mentioned above. I will trace the historical roots of these themes and explore their contemporary relevance for the work of justice.

History

What we now know as confirmation began as a set of ritual actions within a larger, unified rite of initiation. This rite included baptism, continued with a laying on of hands and anointing by the minister, and ended with the celebration of the Eucharist. Over time, the post-baptismal anointing became separated from baptism and Eucharist—giving rise to an independent ritual of "confirmation" in the Christian West. This story of separation explains two different patterns of understanding the sacrament that have marked its history: an early-church emphasis on initiation into the church, and a medieval emphasis on confirmation as a sacrament of maturity and witness.

The Initiation-Church Pattern

The New Testament gives no evidence for the existence of an independent sacrament of confirmation. Catholics once argued that it did, pointing to a story in the Acts of the Apostles. When the apostles Peter and John go to Samaria, they find that the people there have been baptized, but that the Spirit has not yet come upon them. So Peter and John "laid their hands on them, and they received the Holy Spirit" (Acts 8:17). In the context of post-Reformation debates, this text (along with Acts 19:1-7) provided Catholics the proof needed to counter the Reformers' claim that confirmation was unbiblical. Contemporary scholars take a more nuanced (and less polemical) view. If the author of Acts is arguing that something is missing from the Samaritans' baptism, what is missing is not a second *ritual*, but rather

---

[4] Other references to confirmation in the Vatican II documents can be found at: *Lumen Gentium* 26, 33; *Sacrosanctum Concilium* 71; *Apostolicam Actuositatem*, 3; *Ad Gentes* 36; *Presbyterorum Ordinis* 5; *Orientalium Ecclesiarum* 13.

a *relationship* to the wider apostolic church. By laying their hands on the newly baptized, the apostles welcome them into the larger community, which is symbolized by the arrival of the Spirit. Thus these stories are not about confirmation. They are about church.[5]

This theme of the Spirit drawing believers into the church community is evidenced in early patterns of Christian initiation. Within the first few centuries, baptism evolved from a simple water rite into a complex ceremony of prayers, gestures, and symbolic actions. These ceremonies were preceded by an extended period of instruction (the *catechumenate*) meant to prepare the *catechumens* for the radical transition that discipleship implied. Catechumens could be asked to leave behind certain occupations and circles of friends. They were expected to embrace a demanding moral code. The whole process of becoming a follower of Christ meant separating oneself from the common lifestyle and cultural values of the Roman Empire. It meant a transition, a conversion. And the rituals surrounding baptism were meant to evoke this conversion to a new way of life, an alternative vision of reality.

The early rites of initiation varied widely from church to church and from region to region.[6] Well into the fourth and fifth centuries CE, we find considerable diversity of ritual actions between baptism and Eucharist. A number of churches included an anointing with oil after baptism as a way of completing (or "sealing") the water bath. The practice of the church in Rome, however, was unique. Rome included the postbaptismal anointing, but added to it a laying on of hands by the bishop, including a prayer for the Holy Spirit, and a *second* anointing with oil. This distinctive ritual—reserved to the bishop—was the seed that grew into the later sacrament of confirmation.

---

[5] Kenan Osborne cites several biblical scholars who argue along this "baptism-Church axis." See *The Christian Sacraments of Initiation: Baptism, Confirmation, Eucharist* (New York: Paulist Press, 1987), 119.

[6] An excellent study is Maxwell E. Johnson's *The Rites of Christian Initiation: Their Evolution and Interpretation*, rev. ed. (Collegeville, MN: Liturgical Press, 2007). See also Brian D. Spinks, *Early and Medieval Rituals and Theologies of Baptism: From the New Testament to the Council of Trent* (Aldershot: Ashgate, 2006); Aidan Kavanagh, *Confirmation: Origins and Reform* (New York: Pueblo, 1988); Gerard Austin, *Anointing with the Spirit: The Rite of Confirmation* (New York: Pueblo, 1985).

In the early centuries of Christianity, the scale of church was small. Even in Rome, the community was such that the baptismal rites were celebrated together with the bishop, his ministers, and other assistants, surrounded by the whole assembly of the faithful. With the peace of Constantine in 313 and the eventual recognition of Christianity as the religion of the empire later that century, the Christian population grew exponentially and the church spread outward from the cities into the countryside. When the bishop could no longer be present for rituals in outlying communities, his presbyters began to preside in his place. When it came to the rites of initiation, many churches—particularly those in the eastern part of the empire— allowed the presbyter to preside over the entire rite. The church of Rome, however, insisted that, while the presbyter could baptize, the postbaptismal rites should remain reserved to the bishop. In 416 CE, Pope Innocent I argued that when presbyters baptize, they are to refrain from anointing and signing the forehead of the baptized, because "delivering the Holy Spirit" remained the prerogative of the bishop alone.[7]

The Maturity-Mission Pattern

At first, the postbaptismal anointing and laying on of hands were simply postponed until the bishop visited the local community—perhaps even within the same Easter season—at which point he would "confirm" the baptism already administered. As infant baptism became the norm, this "confirmation" was further delayed—occurring in later childhood or adolescence, if at all. Separated from baptism, confirmation drifted free from the rich tangle of biblical imagery that evoked burial and death, resurrection and new birth. The original focus had been on initiation into the church and incorporation into Christ. But when babies entered the body of Christ shortly after birth, what was the meaning of confirmation celebrated years later? Medieval theologians sought to explain the sacrament's continued independent existence. They searched for a theory to explain the ongoing practice.

[7] Johnson, *The Rites of Christian Initiation*, 248.

An early anticipation of the medieval understanding of confirmation can be found as early as the fifth century CE. In a sermon for the feast of Pentecost, Bishop Faustus of Riez (Gaul) described the post-baptismal laying on of hands as a "confirming" act comparable to the descent of the Holy Spirit at Pentecost. He clearly distinguished this rite from baptism: "In baptism we are born anew for life, after baptism we are confirmed for battle (*confirmamur ad pugnam*); in baptism we are washed, after baptism we are strengthened (*post baptismum roboramur*)."[8] These words would make their way into early medieval legal documents and scholastic texts, shaping the way in which theologians came to understand the nature and purpose of confirmation.

Thomas Aquinas adopted this view of confirmation as a spiritual strengthening for battle with the forces of evil and enfolded it into his larger sacramental vision. For Aquinas, God's work through the sacraments conforms to the life of the human person.[9] Just as baptism brings a new birth of the spirit that corresponds to physical birth, so confirmation marks a transition to spiritual adulthood that corresponds to the growing maturity of the individual. For Aquinas and other scholastic theologians, confirmation became a sacrament of mature faith, one which brought an increase in the gifts of the Spirit, strengthening its recipient to publicly profess and defend the faith. The earlier initiation-church pattern, stressing separation *from* the world, gave way to a maturity-mission pattern emphasizing the responsibility to witness *in* the world.

The medieval view took hold. Following the Protestant Reformation, as Catholics turned attention to catechesis, the sacraments were increasingly tied to the educational process. Confirmation coincided with the start of formal catechesis, around age seven (the "age of reason"), while first Communion marked the end, around age eleven or twelve. Up to this point, the traditional sequence of baptism, confirmation, and Eucharist remained, by and large, in place. However, by the eighteenth century, this order began to change. In France, initial

---

[8] Cited in Kavanagh, *Confirmation: Origins and Reform*, 69.

[9] Nathan D. Mitchell, "Dissolution of the Rite of Christian Initiation," in *Made, Not Born: New Perspectives on Christian Initiation and the Catechumenate* (Notre Dame, IN: University of Notre Dame Press, 1976), 64.

catechesis focused increasingly on preparing children for first Communion.[10] Confirmation came later. By the early twentieth century, this local pattern spread with the help of Pope Pius X's decision to lower the official age for first Communion to seven. A novel order became more common: baptism, first penance, first Communion, confirmation. In the United States, confirmation morphed into a kind of graduation ceremony, marking the end of a child's religious education. It bestowed the gifts of the Holy Spirit and offered those graces needed to combat the temptations that were sure to come as one moved from childhood into adolescence and adulthood. The emphasis on strengthening for battle took on greater importance in the face of a culture perceived to be both Protestant and secular. Confirmation made Catholic children "soldiers for Christ" who would combat heresy and sin, and grow to become lay apostles to the world.

The Reforms of Vatican II

Following the liturgical reforms of the Second Vatican Council, the initiation-church pattern and the maturity-mission pattern formed an awkward alliance in Catholic parishes. On the one hand, the earlier initiation-church pattern was recovered, thanks to the council's call for a renewal of the adult catechumenate and its instruction that the Rite of Confirmation was to be revised "so that the intimate connection of this sacrament with the whole of Christian initiation may be shown more clearly" (SC 71). The great achievement on this front was the publication of the revised Rite of Christian Initiation of Adults (RCIA) in 1972. The RCIA reunites all three sacraments of initiation within a single rite, celebrated at the Easter Vigil, with the bishop or priest presiding and the whole community present. In this context, confirmation returns to its original place as a postbaptismal anointing that seals the water bath and moves the newly baptized to the table of the Eucharist.

On the other hand, the medieval maturity-mission pattern survives in the diversity of theological interpretations connected to the revised Rite of Confirmation (1971). This rite, distinct from the RCIA, is intended as a separate ritual for those who were baptized as infants. It

---

[10] Johnson, *The Rites of Christian Initiation*, 382.

remains the most common way in which the sacrament is celebrated today. Following the mandate of the council, this separate rite does strive to connect confirmation to baptism in a number of ways. The candidates are asked to renew their baptismal promises. They are encouraged to use their baptismal names as confirmation names, and, if possible, to have their baptismal godparents as their confirmation sponsors. Alongside this baptismal emphasis is the later language of strengthening and public witness. Indeed, a variety of meanings are juxtaposed within the Rite, but never fully integrated. The suggested message for the bishop's homily is a good example of this unreconciled diversity. Meant to be an opportunity to explain the meaning of confirmation to the candidates, the homily message is supposed to touch on: the experience of Pentecost, the laying on of hands in Acts of the Apostles, the gifts of the Holy Spirit, the death and resurrection of Christ, incorporation into the church, witnessing in the world, charisms, service, vocation, and the renewal of baptism. Maxwell Johnson concludes, "Almost everything we have seen associated with confirmation as a sacrament separate from baptism throughout its long and complex evolution and interpretation is here woven together into one instructional statement."[11]

In the contemporary Catholic Church, there are really two confirmations: (1) a confirmation celebrated in the midst of baptism and Eucharist as part of a single rite, and (2) a confirmation celebrated as a separate rite, held several years after baptism. A vigorous debate has been bubbling for years regarding the proper age for confirmation. In the end, the debate boils down to a more basic theological ambiguity. Is confirmation primarily a sacrament of initiation? Or is confirmation primarily a sacrament of Christian maturity and mission, with its own meaning and its own effects in the life of its recipient? Does the sacrament symbolize the free gift of the Spirit or the personal commitment of the one confirmed? Is it the end of a process of formation or the beginning of a life of faith?

Confirmation and Justice

The theological uncertainty surrounding the sacrament of confirmation is no source for alarm. Indeed, rituals are always rife with

---

[11] Johnson, *The Rites of Christian Initiation*, 406.

ambiguity. They are not empty vessels we imbue with meaning. Rather, meaning emerges out of the concrete celebration of the ritual. By their very nature, Nathan Mitchell reminds us, rites "have *multiple* meanings, an almost inexhaustible *surplus* of meanings." Moreover, rites are *transgressive*: "they inevitably escape and overflow the limits and boundaries that we—their inventors, actants, and 'managers'— invent for them!"[12] Thus, in exploring the implications of confirmation for justice today, we have to attend to the varied meanings that have accrued to the sacrament over history, and to the way in which confirmation is actually experienced in the present.

Spirit, church, and witness—these are the themes that have sprung out of the practice of confirmation over the centuries. Association with the gift of the Spirit goes back to the beginning; initiation into the church community characterized the first centuries; the idea of prophetic witness marked the medieval period; and all three come together in our present experience of the sacrament of confirmation. In an attempt to make sense of the complicated sacrament we have inherited, David Power calls for a "pastoral theology" that, "in the light of sacramental tradition and historical change in the position of the church in culture and society, gives meaning and purpose to this sequence of rites."[13] The following paragraphs offer an initial attempt at such a "pastoral theology," asking how these three themes might encourage a more just way of living within our contemporary consumer culture.

The Gift of the Spirit

The advent of the reign of God was seen by the earliest Christians as the work of the Spirit. Thus it was natural to associate the Spirit with the rites of initiation, which marked the advent of God's reign in the life of an individual. As we have seen, prayers for the Spirit became connected to the postbaptismal anointing and the laying on of hands very early on. Later theologians taught that confirmation

---

[12] Nathan D. Mitchell, "Confirmation in the Second Millennium: A Sacrament in Search of a Meaning," in *La Cresima: Atti del VII Congresso Internazionale di Liturgia*, ed. Ephrem Carr (Rome: Pontificio Ateneo S. Anselmo, 2007), 156.

[13] David N. Power, "Sacraments: Baptism and Confirmation," in *Systematic Theology: Roman Catholic Perspectives*, ed. Francis Schüssler Fiorenza and John P. Galvin (Minneapolis, MN: Fortress Press, 2011), 507.

conferred the fullness of the Holy Spirit, along with the Spirit's gifts of wisdom, understanding, counsel, fortitude, knowledge, piety, and fear of the Lord.

These gifts of the Spirit, the charisms, and the particular graces associated with the sacrament ultimately rest in God's own gift of self. This divine self-donation is what Jesus called the reign of God— God's loving presence to us. The truth of this loving presence is the foundation of Christianity. It finds its definitive expression in Jesus' own life, death, and resurrection. As much as our doctrine and our rituals try to contain or control this self-gift of God, it continually bursts out, flows over, and floods the field of our imagination—challenging all Christians to a radically different way of understanding the world.

God's self-gift flies in the face of our consumer culture. Consumer culture begins with the all-powerful consumer, who freely chooses things. Religion or God can easily become one of these things—something that *I* choose to include in *my* life. But the divine self-gift begins not with the all-powerful consumer but with the all-powerful God, who freely chooses *us*, in order to give God's own self away. This gift of God's love—grace—comes totally undeserved, with no strings attached. We cannot earn it. We cannot pay for it. We cannot "lay it away." We are so shaped by our culture that it can be difficult for us to accept a God who gives so gratuitously, who loves so indiscriminately. This is a God who makes the sun rise on the evil and on the good, who sends rain on the righteous and on the unrighteous; a God who gives the younger son an inheritance he does not deserve, and later welcomes back this wastrel only to throw more money at him; a God who scatters seed all over creation with abandon; a God who pays the guys who worked a few hours the same as those who worked all day. The gift of the Spirit repudiates the tyranny of market-driven economics to decide our fate, instead opening us up to alternative visions of reality.

Confirmation reminds us that God's loving gift of self is what defines our existence. Young people preparing for confirmation are invited to choose a confirmation name, which is often a very personal and meaningful act. The revised rite encourages the candidate to consider using her or his baptismal name. It is not clear that this practice has caught on. If it did, it could serve an important reminder.

While we make a number of choices in our lives, all of these choices—from the frivolous to the profound—rest on a choice we never made: God's decision to bring us into being. Just as I did not choose my own name, so I did not choose my existence. It came as God's first gift to me. Confronting the dehumanizing ramifications of consumer culture begins with this alternative vision. I am not, above all, a consumer or a commodity. I am a gift of God.

Church Community

The identity that God gives to me takes shape within a network of relationships. Christians believe that we grow into a life consonant with the reign of God through our participation in church. Along with choosing a name, candidates for confirmation choose a sponsor—a reminder that none of us is in this alone. The *ecclesial* (from *ekklesia*, "those called," "the church") dimension of the sacrament is key. In the Latin West, the postbaptismal laying on of hands and anointing was reserved to the bishop. This practice may have originated in concerns about power or jurisdiction. It evokes—still to this day—the links between the individual Christian and the larger church. In confirming our baptism, the bishop reminds us that we were not baptized into a little sect or a suburban parish. We were baptized into a worldwide community that takes on flesh in an amazing diversity of cultures and among a remarkable variety of peoples.

We belong to a *universal church*. To be confirmed within a universal church means being called to be in solidarity with all the members of Christ's body, particularly its weakest members. There are over a billion Catholics in the world—the vast majority of whom are poor. The ecclesial tie of confirmation is first a call to solidarity with other Catholics. But that is just a first step toward better understanding the needs and concerns of all people in all parts of the world—Catholic and non-Catholic alike. Our technologically-driven consumer culture complicates the call to such global solidarity. With the internet, cable news, and instant communication, we are more aware of the world's pain than we have ever been before. But we are also increasingly unable to face it. The sheer volume of suffering overwhelms. Over thirty years ago, the German theologian Johann Baptist Metz sadly noted how catastrophes are reported on the radio "in between pieces of music." Quoting Bertolt Brecht, he continued, "When atrocities happen it's like when the rain falls. No one shouts 'stop it!' anymore."[14] In the face of so much suffering, we shut down. We simply do not want to think about it.

Our participation in a local church community ought to school us in solidarity with this universal community. If consumer culture works to keep us isolated from the world's pain, the church should encourage the opposite. The Christian community should draw us into the ongoing process of conversion that was so central to the early process of catechumenate and Christian initiation. One question that every candidate for confirmation should ask is: How does my life within this Christian community differ from a life apart from it? Does the church provide a genuine alternative to life as a consumer in the twenty-first century? I am not advocating for a model of sectarian withdrawal. The church is not an adversary; but it can be an ameliorative, palliative force. The vision is one of "a community of peculiar discourse with practices of memory, hope, and pain that keep healthy human life available in the face of all the 'virtual reality' now on offer in dominant culture."[15]

Prophetic Witness

Talk of justice usually leaps to the task at hand, the call to action. What the presentation here implies is that working for justice (witness) flows out of a particular way of life (church), which in turn finds its source in an alternative vision of reality (Spirit). The gift of the Spirit draws us deeper into the church, so that we might be sent out into the world as prophets of the reign of God.

Walter Brueggemann points to the context out of which prophecy arises. "[S]ome social environments are more hospitable than others to prophets." These environments tend to be "subcommunities that stand in tension with the dominant community in any political economy."[16] Within this "natural habitat," the prophet is formed for two great tasks:

---

[14] Johann Baptist Metz, *Faith in History and Society: Toward a Practical Fundamental Theology*, trans. J. Matthew Ashley (New York: Crossroad, 2011), 157.

[15] Brueggemann, *The Prophetic Imagination*, xvii.

[16] Ibid., xvi.

criticizing and energizing. Starting with the observation that all is not right in the world—children starve, wars rage, the environment deteriorates, while our economic and political structures fuel greater inequality and increased cynicism—the goal is transformation, the movement toward some *alternative*. According to Brueggemann, prophetic witness begins by criticizing the dominant consciousness. It begins by *making known* the deep dysfunctions of our society. The prophet allows the cries of those who are hidden by our consumer culture to be heard. This is a moment of passion and grief. It shatters the numbness of our indifference to the plight of the poor. We need to be moved by those who suffer so that we are moved to act.

The prophet cannot merely criticize; for Bruggemann, the prophet must also energize. Despair sets in motion the fear that nothing will ever change. The problems are too big. There is nothing we can do. The prophet breaks through this despair with God's promise that things will not always be the same. A genuinely new future is possible. By imagining an alternative to the way things are, the prophet offers hope. The prophet presents a vision of life toward which the community might move.

Medieval theologians taught that confirmation strengthens those who have been baptized so that they would be equipped to profess and defend the faith publicly. What might that mean today? Our consumer culture is not out to destroy the faith (if only it took it that seriously!). Rather, consumer culture simply does to faith what it does to *everything*: It transforms it into a meaningless commodity, one more "product" to purchase for those with purchasing power. In the Rite of Confirmation, candidates stand before the bishop and the whole community to proclaim their baptismal vows. This is not a promise to treat the faith as one more item in one's shopping cart or one more app on one's phone. It is a promise to allow the faith to become the orienting framework for one's whole life, and to share this vision with others.

The work of prophetic witness today demands telling the truth about the culture in which we live. Where was my phone made? Who made it and how does that person live? Who harvested the food I eat? How was it shipped? And what is this all doing to the environment? What is my career path? Why am I on it? What drives my desire for advancement, for material comfort, for authority? What guides my political choices? How do I spend my free time? Whom do I admire or emulate? Honestly asking these questions of ourselves may begin to peel back the veneer of our cultural assumptions and allows us a more honest assessment of the world in which we live. Prophetic witness within such a world will require breaking through the numbness of our society's definition of success. It will require breaking through the despair of a life that is ignorant—willfully so—of the suffering of others, so that we might know for ourselves and share with others the good news that there really is another way to live.[17]

Conclusion

When I first started teaching, a group of us young faculty would occasionally gather for lunch to talk about how things were going in the classroom. At one of these lunches, the conversation turned to the difficulty many of us were having getting our students to appreciate the implications of Catholic social teaching. The students liked the idea of social justice but had a hard time imagining how it would have any direct impact on their lives.

In the course of our moaning and groaning about our students, the newest member of the department said, "Yeah, it's all true. But you have to remember, they're only eighteen!"

He didn't mean to be dismissive or paternalistic. It's just that he remembered what it was like *to be* eighteen! He talked about how much he had grown since then, how his own commitments to justice developed gradually over time. Transformation did not take place overnight.

It was an obvious observation, but it struck me. When it comes to the sacraments, our Catholic emphasis on information and education can easily overlook conversion and transformation. Conversion takes time. It is a slow movement from one life to another. The separation of confirmation from baptism and Eucharist was largely a historical accident, and there may be good liturgical and theological reasons for linking them together again. But as long as canon law and pastoral practice keep them separated, the sacraments of initiation will con-

---

[17] Ibid., 117.

tinue to communicate the reality that becoming Christian is a process. And this process does not end at the confirmation ceremony. The gift of the Spirit that makes us church and empowers us for mission continues on. It opens out into a new life, always growing toward the peace and justice of the reign of God. It is this new life that is truly awe-inspiring.

3

Eucharist and Justice

Michael S. Driscoll

Let us begin with a story that drives home the connection between Eucharist and social justice. It concerns a Mass on the border between the United States and Mexico. We have an eyewitness account by Fr. Joe Corpora, CSC. He visited the borderland between Ciudad Juarez, Mexico, and Anapra, New Mexico, on the Feast of All Souls, November 2, 2009. Every Mass is offered for all those who have died trying to cross the border, and the liturgy is celebrated with half the altar on the United States side of the border and the other half on the Mexico side. There is an sixteen-foot-high chain link fence that runs along the border separating the two groups. This wall runs all along the Rio Grande where border patrol trucks and officers stand constant vigil. The scene is dotted with white crosses inscribed with the names of people who have died trying to cross the river. Corpora writes, "I could not stop staring at the fence with the altar on either side. Here we were, gathered as one Body of Christ divided into two. While the Eucharist speaks of our oneness in Christ, of the One Bread and the One Cup, of inclusion, the fence speaks of the opposite—of division and separation and exclusion."[1] The Mass begins as usual, with an entrance procession, but it has to be adjusted given the wall separating the assembly. On both sides of the fence, cross bearers lead the procession followed by the image of Our Lady of Guadalupe, the flags of both countries, and, finally, items people carry when they try to cross—water, food, shoes, a backpack. Corpora continues, "I don't know why, but when I saw the backpack and the shoes I could not stop crying. The Mass was bilingual with beautiful music. Someone read the first reading in Spanish from the Mexico side of the border. Then someone read in English from the U.S. side. I was continually struck by the absurdity of borders. One Body of Christ divided into two."[2] A most moving and pathetic occurrence happens at the Kiss of Peace. People on both sides put their fingers through the chain link fence to touch the fingers of their sisters and brothers on the other side. Fr. Corpora did the same, touching the fingers of another man. He continues, "I cannot describe what I experienced at that moment, perhaps the deepest longing I have ever known for justice, for peace, for unity, for acceptance."[3]

The communion rite was also very powerful. One Bread and One Cup are shared by fellow Catholics on both sides of a fence. Time was allotted after Communion for silent prayer to honor the more than five thousand persons who have died trying to cross the border in the past fifteen years.

> I still cannot put into words all that was in my mind and heart during that Mass, the most moving and powerful Mass I have ever been [*sic*] attended. The picture of one altar divided by a fence with people on both sides of that fence will be forever engraved on my mind and in my heart. May God enlighten and inspire our elected leaders to work for true and real and honest immigration reform.[4]

This story illustrates how the Eucharist at times points to separation and division as much as to communion and unity. In this case, people

---

[1] Joseph V. Corpora, "Concelebrating Mass at the Border," *Notre Dame Magazine* (Autumn, 2010): 45.
[2] Ibid.
[3] Ibid.
[4] Ibid.

celebrate their communion in spite of a wall that separates them. But the Eucharist also moves Christians to a commitment to work for greater unity and for justice in today's world. Until the erection of the wall between Mexico and the United States, the borderlanders (as they like to be called) could move freely back and forth across the border, living their lives and doing their business. Now, families are physically sundered and friends separated by chain-link fences and metal walls. As moving as this eyewitness account is to read, the visual evidence is even more compelling. Thanks to Daniel Groody, CSC, who has produced a documentary film, *One Border, One Body: Immigration and the Eucharist*,[5] we come to a fuller appreciation that sometimes our sacrament of unity and communion ironically points to areas of separation and division. But this sacrament also has the transformative power to shape society and bring about justice in spite of physical separation. Groody writes, "When we look at the experience of migrants today, we see that they are hungry in their homeland, thirsty when they cross the desert, naked after having been robbed even of their clothing, imprisoned in detention centers, sick in hospitals, and then, if they make it across, treated as strangers. I think one of the most powerful ways we can be Catholic is to be hospitable to those who are most vulnerable."[6] The Eucharist presents us with this challenge.

The term "Eucharistic Liturgy" seems commonplace today. Thanks to the Second Vatican Council and a half-century of experience with the reformed Eucharistic Liturgy, Christians, especially Catholics, readily understand this expression. Yet, when you examine the *Baltimore Catechism*, you will not find the term "liturgy"! In the *Baltimore Catechism*, the *de facto* standard Catholic school text in the United States from 1885 to the late 1960s, we find the term "Eucharist" about eighty times and the term "Mass" about twice as often. This chapter looks at various terms in Greek and Latin, such as "Eucharist," "liturgy," and "Mass" with an eye to uncovering the relationship between Eucharist and social justice. What does it mean to be a eucharistic

---

[5] See Daniel G. Groody, "A Theology of Immigration," *Notre Dame Magazine* (Autumn 2004): 48–53; see also http://oneborderonebody.nd.edu/, accessed May 14, 2014.

[6] Daniel G. Groody, "Crossing the Divide: Foundations of a Theology of Migration and Refugees," *Theological Studies* 70, no. 3 (September, 2009): 663.

people? How does the Eucharist implicate us individually and collectively? How does "the breaking of the bread" incite us to action in transforming the world?

The *Baltimore Catechism* makes no explicit reference to social justice, which is not surprising since it was published in 1885, a good six years before Pope Leo XIII promulgated his encyclical letter *Rerum Novarum*, enunciating the social doctrine of the Catholic Church. Since the Second Vatican Council, and especially since the pontificate of John Paul II, there have come to be written a host of documents addressing the rapport between the sacraments and social justice, particularly the Eucharist, oftentimes drawing from writings from the early church in which the link between Eucharist and social justice seemed more apparent.

The question of Eucharist as a sign of unity and the cause of holy Communion is perennial. St. Paul addresses this head-on in his first letter to the community at Corinth, a church dear to Paul, who had visited it and was responsible for proclaiming the Good News there. Corinth was also a very cosmopolitan place, geographically situated at a crossroads, enjoying great cultural diversity, but sometimes creating divisiveness. Paul challenges their eucharistic practice in which the wealthy would come for a eucharistic meal and then, only afterward, allow the poor to share in what was left over. He writes: "The cup of blessing that we bless, is it not sharing in the blood of Christ? The bread that we break, is it not a sharing in the body of Christ? Because there is one bread, we who are many are one body, for we all partake of the one bread" (1 Cor 10:16-17). The church as the body of Christ is one of Paul's favorite analogies: "For just as the body is one and has many members, and all the members of the body, though many, are one body, so it is with Christ. . . . Now you are the body of Christ and individually members of it" (1 Cor 12:12, 27; see parallels in Rom 12:5; Eph 2:16; 4:4; 4:16; and Col 3:15).

During his long papacy, John Paul II underscored the connection between the Eucharist and social justice on many occasions. At the opening of the Year of the Eucharist (October 2004–October 2005), he wrote, "The Eucharist not only provides the interior strength needed for mission, but is also—in some places—*its plan*. For the Eucharist is a mode of being, which passes from Jesus into each Christian, through whose testimony it is meant to spread throughout society and culture."[7] In liturgical circles, this teaching is summarized by the tag "*lex orandi, lex credendi, lex vivendi.*" Prayer (*lex orandi*), particularly liturgical prayer, is given priority in shaping belief (*lex credendi*). Ultimately prayer overflows into Christians living authentically the Gospel (*lex vivendi*). By its very nature Eucharist must respond to the signs of the times. The bishops of the world picked up this theme in preparation for the Episcopal Synod on the Eucharist (2005): "In a culture of death, the Eucharist is the culture of life. In an atmosphere of individual and societal selfishness, the Eucharist reaffirms total self-giving. Where there is hate and terrorism, the Eucharist places love. In response to scientific positivism, the Eucharist proclaims mystery. In desperate times, the Eucharist teaches a sure hope of a blessed eternity."[8]

The words of Jesus "take and eat" primarily signify the gift of himself to us. This gift in turn leads to the fellowship of the table, the unity of the church community and the commitment to share bread with the needy. In the Greek tradition, Eucharist, called *hagia koinonia*, means both Holy Communion and Holy Community. The gifts of bread and wine refer to the great gift of Love, the Eucharist, which spurs charity toward the poorest and to all in need.

What Is in a Name?

There are many names for the celebration of the Eucharist: The Lord's Supper, the Supper of the Marriage of the Lamb, the breaking of the bread, memorial of the passion and resurrection, Holy Sacrifice, Divine Liturgy, Sacred Mysteries, Most Blessed Sacrament, etc. But one name is both very common yet somewhat unusual, namely, the term "Mass." It comes from the Latin *mitto, mittere* meaning to send, and the term is associated with the dismissal rite. The words at the end of the celebration of the Eucharist, *Ite missa est*, bring to mind the

[7] John Paul II, *Mane Nobiscum Domine* (October 7, 2004), 25, http://www.vatican .va/holy_father/john_paul_ii/apost_letters/documents/hf_jp-ii_apl_20041008 _mane-nobiscum-domine_en.html, accessed May 12, 2014.

[8] "The Eucharist: Source and Summit of the Life and Mission of the Church," *Instrumentum Laboris*, Synod of Bishops, XI Ordinary General Assembly (2005), 10, http://www.vatican.va/roman_curia//synod/documents/rc_synod_doc_20050707 _instrlabor-xi-assembly_en.html, accessed May 14, 2014.

missionary mandate of the Risen Lord to his disciples before his Ascension into heaven: "Go therefore and make disciples of all nations" (Matt 28:19). The Latin juridical formula *Ite missa est* originally had no religious meaning. It is somewhat ambiguous in translation but approximates the idea of "The meeting is concluded," or "Go! You are sent." The word "Mass" continues to be used alongside terms such as "Eucharist" and "Liturgy," and it is perfect for developing the idea of mission. In fact, the conclusion of every Mass is immediately linked to being sent forth in mission (derived from the past participle *missus* of the verb *mitto*), a task involving all the baptized, each according to his or her proper vocation in the people of God: bishops, priests, deacons, those in the consecrated life, members of the ecclesial movements, and the laity. Bearing witness is essential in fulfilling this mission. It is the first duty of every Christian sent forth into the world. The Eucharist is the pulsating heart of mission, its authentic source, and its only end.

The dismissal at Mass is an invitation to mission. The eucharistic goal is to make us grow in the love of Christ and his desire to bring the Gospel to everyone. "These few words succinctly express the missionary activity of the church. The People of God might be helped to understand more clearly this essential dimension of the church's life, taking the dismissal as the starting point."[9]

The word "Mass," and the expression "Eucharistic Liturgy," are often used interchangeably. Let us then explore these words separately: Eucharist and Liturgy. The mystery of the Eucharist is placed as the true center of the Christian life. In fact, *Sacrosanctum Concilium* (the Constitution on the Sacred Liturgy) from the Second Vatican Council calls it the source and the summit of the life of the church (SC 10). It is no wonder that so much has been written on the subject of the Eucharist from many different perspectives!

The term "Eucharist" itself is from the Greek verb *eucharistein* meaning "to give thanks." Although this thanksgiving refers specifically to the prayer said over the bread and the wine, the attitude of thanksgiving prevails in Christian prayer and in all of life. The prayer

---

[9] Benedict XVI, *Sacramentum Caritatis*, Post-Synodal Apostolic Exhortation (2007), 51, http://www.vatican.va/holy_father/benedict_xvi/apost_exhortations/documents/hf_ben-xvi_exh_20070222_sacramentum-caritatis_en.html, accessed May 12, 2014.

of thanksgiving is always addressed to the Father for everything accomplished in creation, for our redemption in Christ, and our continuous sanctification by the Holy Spirit. The form of the eucharistic prayer is the church's prayer of blessing, whereby we express our thanksgiving for all God's benefits.

We find in liturgy a beautiful reflection of the Eucharist in the Common Preface IV: "It is truly right and just, our duty and our salvation, always and everywhere to give you thanks [*eucharistein*], Lord, holy Father, almighty and eternal God. For, although you have no need of our praise, yet our thanksgiving [*eucharistia*] is itself your gift, since our praises add nothing to your greatness but profit us for salvation, through Christ our Lord." [10] All the prefaces leading into the Holy, Holy, Holy and the eucharistic prayer are a mini-Eucharist as they all begin with giving thanks to God. But this particular preface underscores that it is we who benefit from this act of thanksgiving as the Eucharist instills in us deep-felt gratitude that leads to the praise of God.

The link between Eucharist and social justice, implicit in the term "Mass," has become more explicit in the teachings of the church. Beginning especially with John Paul II, continuing throughout the papacy of Benedict, and still dear to the thought of Pope Francis, the implicit connection between Eucharist and ethics has been made more explicit. The Eucharist empowers the choices and the ethical and moral behavior of believers, affecting philosophy, art, literature, and even civil and legal institutions, contributing to fashioning the features of an entire civilization, in personal and family life as well as in cultural, political, and social life. The Eucharist moves Christians to a commitment to justice in today's world. In the words of Pope Francis, "There is always the risk that some moments of prayer can become an excuse for not offering one's life in mission; a privatized lifestyle can lead Christians to take refuge in some false forms of spirituality." [11]

---

[10] International Commission on English in the Liturgy, 2010.

[11] Francis, Apostolic Exhortation *Evangelii Gaudium* (The Joy of the Gospel), 262, Libreria Editrice Vaticana: http://w2.vatican.va/content/francesco/en/apost_exhortations/documents/papa-francesco_esortazione-ap_20131124_evangelii-gaudium.html, accessed May 12, 2014.

John Paul II insisted on the point that Eucharist finds its authenticity in communal sharing. "It is the impulse which the Eucharist gives to the community for *a practical commitment to building a more just and fraternal society*. In the Eucharist our God has shown love in the extreme, overturning all those criteria of power which too often govern human relations and radically affirming the criterion of service." [12] We need only look at Jesus' words, "Whoever wants to be first must be last of all and servant of all" (Mark 9:35), and, more important, his actions (such as feet-washing in John 13:1-20) to discover the profound meaning of Eucharist that calls us to service.

Liturgy is another term with which we have become familiar over the past half-century. In times past, this term was confined to Orthodox Christian circles, but now it is widely used and understood by Christians everywhere. The term is biblical, and the writers of the early church employed it often. Paul uses the word *leitourgia* in 2 Corinthians 9:12. In classical Greek, this is a word with a noble history, derived from *laos*, meaning people, and *ergon*, meaning work. There has been a tendency to translate this term, then, as the work of the people. But in so doing, we leave God out of the equation. The term *leitourgia* is better rendered as a public work—both God's and ours.

In the great days of Athens, some generous citizens volunteered to shoulder out of their own pockets the expenses of enterprises in which the city was engaged. It might be to defray the expenses of training the chorus for a new drama or a team to compete for the honor of the city in the games; it might be to pay for the outfitting and manning of a trireme or man-of-war in times of the city's peril. A *leitourgia* was originally a service of the state voluntarily accepted. For Christians, giving is something that should be volunteered. It should be accepted as a privilege to help in some way the household of God.

St. John Chrysostom, the fourth-century priest from Antioch who became archbishop of the imperial capital at Constantinople, speaks about *leitourgia* in the larger sense. One recurring feature of his homilies is his emphasis on care for the needy. Echoing themes found in

---

[12] John Paul II, Apostolic Letter *Mane Nobiscum Domine*, 28, http://www.vatican.va/holy_father/john_paul_ii/apost_letters/documents/hf_jp-ii_apl_20041008_mane-nobiscum-domine_en.html, accessed May 12, 2014.

the Gospel of Matthew, he calls on the rich to lay aside materialism in favor of helping the poor, often employing his considerable rhetorical skills to shame wealthy people to abandon conspicuous consumption: "It is not possible for one to be wealthy and just at the same time. Do you pay such honor to your excrements as to receive them into a silver chamber pot when another man made in the image of God is perishing in the cold?"[13]

Commenting on 2 Corinthians 9:1-15, Chrysostom notes the connection between service and ministry, which is referred to as a liturgy. But he insists that Eucharist must be translated into helping the poor. For him, helping the poor is just as much a liturgy as celebrating the Eucharist. Elsewhere he writes,

> Do you wish to honor the Body of Christ? Do not ignore Him when he is naked. Do not pay homage in the temple clad in silk—only then to neglect Him outside where He suffers cold and nakedness. He who said, "This is my body" is the same One who said, "You saw Me hungry and you gave Me no food" and "Whatever you did for the least of My brothers, you did also for Me." What good is it if the Eucharistic Table is overloaded with golden chalices, when He is dying of hunger? Start by satisfying His hunger, and then, with what is left, you may adorn the altar as well. The temple of our afflicted neighbor's body is more holy than the altar of stone on which you celebrate the holy sacrifice. You are able to contemplate this altar everywhere, in the street and in the open squares.[14]

The Lord's Day and Mission

The Lord's Day is among other things the day of solidarity and sharing with the poor, insomuch as the Eucharist is the bond of fellowship and the source of communion. Beginning with the Sunday Mass, a tide of charity flows from the praying assembly into the whole

[13] J. H. W. G. Liebeschuetz, *Barbarians and Bishops: Army, Church, and State in the Age of Arcadius and Chrysostom* (Oxford: Clarendon Press, 1990), 176.

[14] St. John Chrysostom, *In Evangelium S. Mattaei, hom.* 50.3–4; PG 58:508–9; cf. John Paul II, Encyclical Letter *Sollicitudo Rei Socialis*, December 30, 1987, 31, http://www.vatican.va/holy_father/john_paul_ii/encyclicals/documents/hf_jp-ii_enc_30121987_sollicitudo-rei-socialis_en.html, accessed June 4, 2014; and in his Encyclical Letter *Ecclesia de Eucharistia*, April 17, 2003, 34, http://www.vatican.va/holy_father/special_features/encyclicals/documents/hf_jp-ii_enc_20030417_ecclesia_eucharistia_en.html, accessed June 4, 2014.

world. The Eucharist prepares the church for mission. It is the authentic source of mission and its only end. The Eucharist is the "source and the summit" (*fons et culmine*) of the Christian life as it is expressed in the daily lives of those who break bread together as Jesus commanded. If prayer (*lex orandi*) shapes belief (*lex credendi*), then together they find their true authentication in genuine Christian living (*lex vivendi*). To ignore this inner connection between Eucharist and life is to ignore the bond between the life and mission of the church.

We read in the Synoptic Gospels that on the night before Jesus died, he took bread, said the blessing, broke it, and gave it to his disciples. These four verbs (taking, blessing, breaking, and giving) became associated with the fourfold action of the Eucharist. The second action—blessing—is that from which we get the name Eucharist, here meaning the blessing. The fourfold action must have been so familiar to the early church that in other meal stories these verbs are used as a veiled reference to the Eucharist. For example, in the story of the multiplication of the loaves and the fishes, as well as the meal with the disciples at Emmaus, these four verbs appear. Anyone steeped in the prayer of the early church would have been struck by the similarity with the Last Supper. This fourfold action, therefore, gave shape to the second part of the Mass, the Liturgy of the Eucharist, where bread is taken (presentation of the gifts), blessed (the entire eucharistic prayer), broken (fraction rite accompanied by the "Lamb of God" litany), and distributed (the communion rite).

Yet one of the earliest names given to the Eucharist is derived from the third action—"the breaking of the bread." We read in the Acts of the Apostles, for example, that the early community "devoted themselves to the apostles' teaching and fellowship, to the breaking of bread and the prayers. . . . All who believed were together and had all things in common; they would sell their possessions and goods and distribute the proceeds to all, as any had need. Day by day, as they spent much time together in the temple, they broke bread at home" (Acts 2:42, 44-46). Certainly this rite of bread breaking is another way of speaking about the Eucharist. It finds its clearest expression in the mutual sharing implied by breaking and sharing bread with another person. It is not surprising, then, that we find this expression in Luke's account of the post-resurrection appearance of Christ to the two disciples at Emmaus. They did not recognize Christ until he sat at table with them. He took bread, blessed it, broke it, and gave it to them to eat. Luke emphasizes that they came to recognize Jesus as the Christ in the "breaking of the bread." This type of remembering is not a psychological recall. It implies something much greater. When the prefix *ana* precedes the word "to remember" (*mnesis*), it intensifies its meaning. *Anamnesis* is a kind of remembering in a most intense way. We find traces of this in the Jewish Passover celebration, in which the participants share a special meal. All the food elements are specially prepared and each food recalls certain events of the history of Israel. In this way we might say the participants eat their history. It was and still is a wonderful and ingenious way to transmit religious tradition to children. But in this context it is not a simple remembrance of past events. Rather, past events are recalled because they are presently meaningful. The past becomes present in the ritual action. In a way, past events are rendered present in the act of remembering. Or, we might look at it from another angle and say that the participants become present to the past in the act of sharing the Passover meal together.

Each time we invoke the Lord's Prayer, we reference the bread and its ethical implications. " 'Give us this day our daily bread' obliges us to do everything possible in cooperation with international, state, and private institutions to end or at least reduce the scandal of hunger and malnutrition. . . . The Christian laity, formed at the school of the Eucharist, are called to assume their specific political and social responsibilities."[15]

All the sacraments, but especially the Eucharist, emphasize the role of the Holy Spirit. Liturgically, this is symbolized by imposing hands over the gifts or the people and praying that the Holy Spirit may descend. We are so confident that the Holy Spirit is present to the church as promised by Christ after his resurrection that we use the imperative form of the verb "Send forth your Spirit." We also recognize that the Spirit moves where the Spirit wills. We do not control the Holy Spirit. Rather, we are controlled by God's Spirit. There are many ways in which the Spirit of God moves in our lives. In the Constitution on the Liturgy, several different modes of real presence were delineated, for example, when two or more are gath-

---

[15] Benedict XVI, Post-Synodal Apostolic Exhortation *Sacramentum Caritatis* (2007), 91, http://www.vatican.va/holy_father/benedict_xvi/apost_exhortations/documents /hf_ben-xvi_exh_20070222_sacramentum-caritatis_en.html, accessed May 12, 2014.

ered in Christ's name to pray, to sing the psalms, to work together for the coming of the kingdom. But the Eucharist is the sacrament of Christ's presence par excellence, precisely due to the sanctifying work of the Spirit in our midst.

The calling forth of the Holy Spirit for transformation in liturgical rites is called the *epiclesis* (from *klesis*, "invocation," and *epi*, "over or from above"). In the Eucharist there is a double *epiclesis*. In the first case, the Holy Spirit is invoked to transform the gifts of bread and wine into the body and blood of Christ. In the second instance, the Spirit is called down (implicitly if not explicitly) to transform the assembly so that we may become that which we receive. Eucharist, then, is not only *what* is on the altar but also *who* is at the altar. All the baptized are called to become bread broken for the world and wine poured out for others. The social justice implications of this action are profound.

It is the communion (both of those in community and what is received) that comprehends the ethical dimension of the Eucharist. Holy Communion makes demands on all those who communicate. It obliges all who receive to care for the needs of the entire church. By our sharing in the one bread and the one cup, we are to become that which we celebrate. In receiving the body and blood of Christ we must recognize Christ in the poorest, the outcasts of society, the oppressed. St. Augustine writes:

> If you are the body and members of Christ, then it is your sacrament that is placed on the table of the Lord; it is your sacrament that you receive. To that which you are you respond "Amen" ("yes, it is true!") and by responding to it you assent to it. For you hear the words, "the Body of Christ" and respond "Amen." Be then a member of the Body of Christ that your Amen may be true.[16]

Banqueting has long been used to speak of communion with God. In Psalm 23, for example, we see the Good Shepherd as preparing a banquet. In the story of Lazarus and the rich man, the banquet image predominates in speaking of afterlife. The meal has long been associated with the heavenly banquet. It is not surprising that in the ancient world, afterlife was compared to a banquet. We find this imagery in both Christian and pagan writings and funerary decoration. In the

---

[16] St. Augustine, *Sermo* 272; PL 38:1247.

Christian use of the banquet symbol, we stress that what we do here and now in this life is a foretaste of the celestial banquet. It is at the same time already accomplished in this world through the cross of Christ and the work of the Holy Spirit, but not completely fulfilled. We live in a time of the "already, but not yet." Early Christian liturgy understood this dimension when they would sing the Aramaic expression "Maranatha." This acclamation was intentionally ambiguous because it could mean simultaneously "The Lord has come" and "Come, Lord!" It pointed to the fact that the Lord has already made his appearance in human history but that we await his return in glory. We live in the period between the two comings of the Christ, the "anointed one," the Messiah. Again St. Paul points to this dimension of the "already, but not yet" when he writes, "For as often as you eat this bread and drink the cup, you proclaim the Lord's death until he comes!" (1 Cor 11:26). It is this dimension that renews our hope in the imperfectness of the world. Knowing that we will never achieve perfect justice in this world does not dispense us from working for a more just world. In the Eucharist we proclaim our faith of that which has already happened, we look with hope to the future of a world which is yet to come, and we live currently in the love of Christ, the living agape of God.

We have numerous ways to speak about the church as Christ's Mystical Body, about the vine and the branches, about the communion of saints. But Christ himself has given us the example regarding service. For he said that a glass of water given to a beggar was given to him. He made heaven hinge on the way we act toward him in disguise of commonplace, frail, ordinary humanity.

> Did you give me food when I was hungry?
> Did you give me drink when I was thirsty?
> Did you give me clothes when my own were all rags?
> Did you come to see me when I was sick, or in prison, or in trouble?

And to those who say that they never had a chance to do such a thing, that they lived two thousand years too late, he will say again what they had the chance of knowing all their lives, that if these things were done for the very least of the brethren, they were done to him.

4

Penance and Justice

Doris Donnelly

Laura Hillenbrand tells a riveting story of forgiveness in her book *Unbroken*.[1] She writes about Louis (Louie) Zamperini, "a one boy insurgency in his youth," from Torrance, California, who developed into a world-class runner with prospects to win gold at the 1940 Olympics. When the Second World War derailed his dream, Louie ended up in the Pacific theatre, dropping bombs from a quirky, defective B24 plane that one pilot described as "sitting on the front porch and flying the house." When an engine gave out, Zamperini and one other crew member landed in the ocean, where, for forty-seven days—a record for survival at sea—they dealt with hunger, dementia, and expectant sharks bumping underneath and alongside their fragile raft. Rain slaked their desperate thirst; albatrosses that unexpectedly perched on the raft became their occasional sustenance. They traveled two thousand miles before they were spotted by a Japanese bomber, captured, and then interred in a series of brutal POW camps.

---

[1] Laura Hillenbrand, *Unbroken* (New York: Random House, 2010). For the passages about Louis Zamperini's experience of forgiveness, see 372–80.

Zamperini was singled out as a celebrity by a psychopathic guard named Mutsuhiro Watanabe, also known as the "Bird," for an unrelenting regime of torture: starvation, slave labor, medical experiments, clubbing with a Kendo stick and baseball bat, whippings to the head with his metal belt buckle, and the repeated humiliation of having his face mushed into feces.

A few POWs, Zamperini among them, escaped execution by the Japanese at the war's end, but his reentry to life as he once knew it was not smooth. The loving family he left behind and a new wife, Cynthia Applewhite, were not enough to keep the demons at bay. Alcoholism, nightmares, flashbacks, and rage consumed him; risky investments that didn't pan out left the couple and their baby daughter penniless. In rare lucid moments, Louie was obsessed with returning to Japan to find and kill the Bird. At her wits end, Cynthia prepared for divorce but had second thoughts after attending a Billy Graham crusade. She enticed, begged, cajoled, and finally tricked Louie into joining her. Begrudgingly, Louie took a seat in one of the last rows as Billy Graham scanned his audience and began. "Here tonight," Graham said, "there's a drowning man, a drowning woman, lost in the sea of life." Graham spoke passionately of God reaching into the world with tangible blessings and one promise above all: "God gives strength to outlast our sorrows."

Sorrowful memories flooded Zamperini: the raft salvaged from the plane, the desperate nights at sea, the Japanese bomber overhead riddling them with bullets, the hellish camps, and the Bird. Graham paused and then extended the invitation to everyone to give their lives to Christ. "God has spoken to you. You come on." Come on down. Give your fears, your worries, and your life to Christ. Louie was transfixed. It was too much for him to absorb. He bolted from his seat and headed for the exit just as Graham commanded that "No one is to leave. You can leave while I'm preaching but not now." Louie turned around, followed Graham's voice, and surrendered all that he was, all that he had, to Christ.

When Louie and Cynthia returned home, Louie poured his whiskey cache into the sink and slept without nightmares or flashbacks for the first time in five years. His war was over. He was a new creation, no longer in the grip of revenge, fear, humiliation, and helplessness. A shift occurred within him. He named it "forgiveness, beautiful and effortless and complete."

It was a major turnaround, a conversion that urged Louie to redress the power of evil and to act in concrete ways to restore justice to a past where injustice reigned with impunity. The extravagant forgiveness he accepted and that "saved" him in turn beckoned him to extend forgiveness to others. It was not difficult to decide where to begin the reparation. A visit to Japan was high on the list. Louie began undoing the damage of war by sharing peace with his former guards during a 1950 visit to the Sugamo camp in Japan. "In bewilderment," Hillebrand writes, "the men who had abused him watched him come to them, his hands extended, a radiant smile on his face."

Instinctively, Louie Zamperini understood that forgiveness was a two-way street, that forgiveness, once received, has to be passed on; that, as improbable as it seemed, the initiative of forgiving began with the one injured and not, as one might expect, with the one causing injury; and that the trip to Sugamo was a powerful symbolic act: although it neither condoned or erased the evil Louie Zamperini lived through, it allowed a profound healing to take place.

Justice is God's order for the world. Louie's symbolic gesture of extending forgiveness did not restore God's order completely, but it tilted the scales of justice in favor of God's grace.

The reciprocity and the power at the heart of Louie Zamperini's story have the Lord's Prayer as their antecedent: we ask to be forgiven as we forgive others. Some of us, probably all of us, hope that God doesn't take us at our word and that God forgives us with far greater compassion, gentleness, mercy, and speed than the forgiveness we offer to others. But even if it is an ideal, the reciprocal model represents a justice claim: we cannot make a better world, a more peaceful world, a world where relationships are healed, without imitating the forgiveness of Christ that we find front and center in the New Testament.

The Early Church and Canonical Penance[2]

The forgiveness of Jesus Christ permeates the Christian Gospel. Jesus not only preached but also practiced forgiveness. In one of his last conscious recorded activities, Jesus wrestled with the experience

---

[2] Two especially helpful books on the history of penance are Joseph Martos, *Doors to the Sacred* (New York: Doubleday, 1981), and some essays in a small book edited

of forgiving his executioners: "Father, forgive them; they do not know what they are doing" (Luke 23:34). Far from being an isolated reference, the Gospel of Jesus frequently returns to the theme of forgiveness and teaches in words and behavior that this response is what it means to be a follower of Christ. For Jesus, forgiveness is a restorative event. Forgiveness restores relationships that are displaced, broken, or destroyed and allows for the events of human life, even when they turn out badly, not to be beyond repair.

The early church proclaimed baptism for the forgiveness of sins. Converts to Christianity submitted to a lengthy spiritual journey before they were submerged in the waters of baptism and were born again. Because the rites of initiation were so rigorous, vetting of candidates so comprehensive, and the commitment to a new life in Christ so total, the possibility that Christians might renege on their baptismal promises by sinning again seems not to have occurred to leaders of the community.

When the early church eventually faced postbaptismal sin, two approaches emerged. On the one hand, those whose focus was to preserve an unblemished body of Christ favored a "one strike and you're out" policy. This hard-line approach held three sins in particular— murder, apostasy, and adultery—to be so heinous, so destructive of community, that readmission to the fold was unthinkable.

Contrarily, and perhaps counterintuitively, there were those who recognized that Jesus not only railed against sin but also was lavish in extending mercy and forgiveness. No sin was beyond God's mercy and largesse, and thus the community ought to follow that example. Of interest is that the pericope in John 8:1-11—the forgiveness of the woman taken in adultery—was one of the last additions to the Gospel of John, which also was the last of the gospels in the canon of the Scriptures as we know it. The consensus is that the story was placed there, last but not least, to reinforce that even adultery, once considered unforgivable by the early followers, would have been forgiven by Jesus and ought to be the model for the Christian community as well.

As early as 100, the idea of readmitting sinners after baptism was in the air (and on parchment). A document identified as *The Shepherd*

---

by Carra de Vaux Saint-Cyr, et al., *The Sacrament of Penance* (Glen Rock, NJ: Paulist Press, 1966).

of Hermas hinted at such a possibility, but only once in a lifetime, and only after a strenuous reckoning. Tertullian called it the "second plank after shipwreck" (*De Paenitentia*, 4, 2), a creative and imaginative way of expressing both the seriousness of sin as shipwreck, the plank of wood as a saving grace, and the image of the ship itself as the home of the Christian community.

Gradually, the practice of a second chance took hold. It would not be the last time that a rite connected with ecclesial penance and forgiveness would be adapted to the times. Justice was at stake—God's order for the world had been compromised by serious sin and had to be addressed. The process unfolded thusly: Confession was made to the bishop or his designated representative and was private; clearly, in a small community where everyone knew everyone else's business, and where the sins in question were notorious, it was no surprise when the sin became known. The bishop assessed the seriousness of the confessed sin and, if appropriate, enrolled the person in the Order of Penitents.[3] The process could include a ritual of signing with ashes and exclusion of the penitent from eucharistic worship. A penance was imposed and could last for days, months, or years; it was expected to be performed before absolution and certainly before readmission to eucharistic worship. There were also aftereffects for the penitent to accept—exile, if one was guilty of murder; abstaining from sexual intercourse, if one was guilty of adultery or fornication, whether one was married or not; and exclusion from certain professions, among them, most prominently, the priesthood.

The practice of being restored onto the mother ship was not for the fainthearted. Thus, when Fabiola, a citizen of Rome, decided to repent of her sins, she followed a common but arduous procedure. This is the scene described by St. Jerome:

> On the day before the Pasch, when the whole city was looking on, Fabiola took her place in the ranks of the penitents . . . with disheveled hair, a ghastly countenance, soiled hands and sordid neck. She prostrated herself before the bishop, the presbyters and all the people, as they wept along with her. . . . She laid bare to all her wound, and a Rome in tears beheld a livid scar on her flesh. The sides of her garment were unfastened, her head was bared, her lips

---

[3] For a fine study on the Order of Pentinents, see Joseph Favazza, *The Order of Penitents: Historical Roots and Pastoral Future* (Collegeville, MN: Liturgical Press, 1987).

tightly drawn. She did not enter the church of the Lord, but like Miriam, the sister of Moses, she sat apart, outside the camp, in order that the priest who had cast her forth might personally call her back again.[4]

Fabiola may have confessed her sins to the bishop in private, but she certainly worked out her penance in public. The penances imposed were severe by contemporary standards: Jerome's summary indicates that Fabiola was called on to wear a penitent's garb of sackcloth, that she purposely left her hair disheveled and rubbed ashes on her face, and that she chastised her body, communicating to all an interior state of compunction to complement what they saw on the outside. The text reveals not only that the community witnessed Fabiola's mortifications but also that well-wishers commiserated and wept with her.

Other early documents provide evidence that bishops urged their congregations to "colabor" with penitents, to do penance on their behalf, and that members of the community, clergy included, did so. The community was also frequently involved in recommending to the bishop those penitents who had suffered enough, whose contrition seemed genuine, and whose tears seemed sincere. Those who approached their satisfactions with indifference or for questionable motives could be sure the congregation would consider it their solemn duty to report infractions and inappropriate conduct to the bishop. In both cases, it could be expected that the congregation would be heard.

It is worth noting that Fabiola's penance and the satisfaction for her sins took place before absolution. Only when the community was assured by her external behaviors that an interior sorrow burned deep in her heart would the report to the bishop be favorable. She endured a difficult journey, but we can also imagine how relieved Fabiola was that a second plank after shipwreck was available at all and that her salvation was once again possible.

---

[4] St. Jerome's description of the Penance of Fabiola, recorded in the *Gelasian Sacramentary*, Epist. 77, *To Oceanus* (PL 22, 692), is cited, in translation, by Paul Palmer, *Sacraments and Forgiveness*, Sources of Christian Theology, vol. 2 (Westminster: The Newman Press, 1959), 121.

Not everyone was as courageous or as eager as Fabiola to submit to canonical penance as it was practiced in the early church, and for at least three reasons it fell into disuse. First, it certainly was demanding. The penances were difficult and required an almost superhuman humility, not only to acknowledge one's sinfulness, but also to accept mortifications in full view of everyone. Second, there was the stigma of having been enrolled in the Order of Penitents. A separate class of citizenship was automatically attached to those who sinned seriously enough to abrogate their baptismal commitment. The aftereffects carried a lifetime sentence of penances to help not sinning again.

Third, since a "once only" rule prevailed, it seemed more sensible to postpone penance for old age or one's deathbed. To use up the one-time opportunity while a person was young seemed reckless. No matter how sincere the confession, no matter how ardent the contrition, no matter how disposed a person might be to submit to public penance, it was always possible that one could sin again. Then what? Understandably, Christians were nervous about taking such a risk and being damned forever.

Not only penitents but also some bishops were sensitive to the issue of recurrent sin, and a few of them discouraged the young from submitting to canonical penance. There was, of course, the consoling message that, while the church could not absolve those who sinned repeatedly, it was always possible to plead one's case with God, should death occur before a person took advantage of the Rite. Nonetheless, ranks of the faithful at Eucharist dwindled. The time was right for a new penitential discipline. It came from the Irish church.

Penance in the Middle Ages

The new penitential model was indebted to the monastic practice of disclosing the state of one's soul, including one's sins, to an abbot. The disclosure happened routinely as part of a monk's life—monthly, or even weekly, in some settings. Its goal was to gain knowledge of one's self, a precondition to growth in love of God and neighbor. The monks grafted their experience onto a penitential discipline available to everyone. And it caught on.

Under the direction of the Irish monks, the new ritual of penance extended to all sins, both great and small, and could be repeated more than once in a lifetime. It no longer took place in the public arena but developed as a private act. A person confessed to and was counseled by a monk—or sometimes by a "spiritual friend"—who provided instruction pertinent to the life of the penitent, assigned a penance, and granted absolution before the penance was completed. Because the variety of sins dealt with every conceivable infringement of law, confessors were aided by penitential books that catalogued sins with carefully graded penalties according to the particular estimate of the gravity of the offense. For example, on the matter of gluttony, the author of the Penitential of Cummean wrote: "He who suffers excessive distention of the stomach and the pain of satiety shall do penance for one day. If he suffers to the point of vomiting, though he is not in the state of infirmity, he [shall do] penance for seven days."[5]

The "tariff" penance introduced by the Irish monks placed the community in the background and also altered an understanding of sin. Sin became a private matter. The penitential books, setting down as they did satisfaction required for particular sins, emphasized a legalistic, objective appraisal of the penitent's condition. Sin was thus regarded not as an inner reality with social repercussions but as an objective act, the seriousness of which was ascertainable by consulting penitential books. Genuine contrition remained an essential ingredient in canonical penance, but juridicism flavored the experience.

Although the Irish penitentials were abandoned by the late Middle Ages, their juridical orientation was reinforced in subsequent centuries. Once the practice of repeated private confession to a priest was established at the Fourth Lateran Council in 1215 as an official sacrament in Western Christianity, theologians at European universities parsed issues connected with the sacrament. What was the role of the priest? Was it to assure penitents that their sins were forgiven because of their contrition? It seemed to be a debatable point since the imprecatory form of absolution ("May God, in his mercy, forgive you your sins") was changed to a declaratory version ("I absolve you from your sins"). When, then, did the remission of sins occur? Was the effective cause of being released from sin a contrite heart with

---

[5] John T. McNeill and Helena M. Gamer, *Medieval Handbooks of Penance* (New York: Octagon Books, 1965), 101.

which one approached the sacrament, or was it in the words of absolution spoken by the priest?

Thomas Aquinas, the master theologian-philosopher of the scholastic period, proposed contrition as unquestionably necessary, but so too was the grace enveloped in the confession itself, in the words of absolution that provided an encounter with mercy dispensed through Christ's church.[6] Thomas trusted Christ's promise that the power to bind and loose sins was entrusted to the church, but along with it, he understood that without the personal investment of sorrow for sin, the sacrament would be defective.

Not everyone agreed with Thomas. John Duns Scotus, for one, identified a loophole in his argument, and it focused on contrition. Two kinds of contrition had been identified—perfect contrition, elicited by a pure love of God and a detestation of sin, and imperfect contrition, motivated by fear of hell and eternal damnation. Scotus agreed that it was possible for perfect contrition to merit God's forgiveness without the sacrament of penance, but would this not be a rare occurrence? Who would be so bold to acknowledge such perfection and to stake one's salvation on it? To be secure, it was better to assume one's contrition as imperfect and to approach the sacrament. Safety thus hinged on the words of absolution spoken by the priest.[7]

Future generations would privilege the pastoral and theological wisdom of Thomas's balanced approach, but in practice, a preoccupation with the words of absolution defined the moment when sin, and the punishment due to it, was remitted.

The Reformers of the sixteenth century acknowledged repentance as an essential part of Christian life but critiqued the sacrament of penance as without biblical foundation and as an exercise of the papacy to control, and interfere, with Christ's mercy. Still, Martin Luther vacillated about penance as a sacrament in his "Babylonian Captivity of the Church," denouncing its abuses but commending its

---

[6] That contrition informed by love is the only true repentance and alone remits sin is an idea that dominates the theology of Thomas Aquinas. See *Summa Contra Gentiles*, 4, 72; *Summa Theologica*, III, q. 86, a. 2.

[7] John Duns Scotus, *On the Sentences*, 4, dist. 14, q. 4, numbers 6, 7; dist. 19, q. I, n. 24 (*Opera*, 92, 382).

practice in the same document.[8] For those who wished private confession, John Calvin, among other Reformers, had no objection.[9]

The Council of Trent[10] set the parameters for the sacrament that influenced its practice for centuries. The sacrament comprised three essential elements: contrition, confession, and satisfaction. Contrition was the *sine qua non*. Confession required itemizing each serious, or mortal, sin—what kind, how often, and with any extenuating circumstances. Deliberately concealing a mortal sin invalidated the confession; accidentally omitting a mortal sin required its denunciation in a forthcoming confession. In his role as judge, the priest needed evidence before counseling, and in some instances reprimanding, as well as assigning a penance which was, in any case, far lighter than those in earlier periods, consisting, as it did, of prayers or some devotional exercise.

Not much changed in the ensuing centuries. Catholic practice up to the mid-twentieth century involved long lines for confession in churches on Saturdays, especially in days preceding the feasts of Christmas and Easter. The obligation to confess mortal sins during the Easter season was assumed as the "Easter Duty" by all Catholics. At the same time, influenced by debates about personal freedom and vagaries of human motivation, Catholics began to question whether eating meat on Friday, generally understood as a mortal sin, merited eternal damnation by a loving God. An increasingly educated Catholic laity in the United States, Europe, and elsewhere, also became aware of sins that warranted attention but were not listed in

---

[8] Martin Luther, "The Babylonian Captivity of the Church," in *Luther's Works* vol. 36, American ed. (Philadelphia: Fortress Press, 1959).

[9] John Calvin, *Institutes of Christian Religion*, vol. 1, book 3 (Philadelphia: Presbyterian Board of Christian Education, n.d.), xiv. Curiously, over the years, Protestant pastors and theologians have written exquisitely about the need and value of auricular confession—Max Thurian and Dietrich Bonhoeffer come to mind—while some current Lutheran and Presbyterian theologians and pastors have revived the practice in their congregations at the same time that there is a decline of the practice among Roman Catholics. See Max Thurian, *Confession* (London: SCM Press, 1958), and Dietrich Bonhoeffer, *Life Together* (New York: HarperOne, 2009).

[10] The Decrees and Canons of the Council of Trent may be found in their entirety in Denzinger-Bannwart, *Enchiridion symbolorum, definitionum et declarationum de rebus fidei et morum*, 30th ed. (Freiburg: Umberg-Rahner, 1954); a selection of pertinent texts are provided by Paul Palmer, *Sacraments and Forgiveness*, 237–54.

"Examination of Conscience" pamphlets available in the vestibules of churches.[11] Personal culpability for missing Mass on Sunday paled in comparison to social sins, including racism and sexism that excluded neighbors from employment and educational opportunities, or when federal or local budgets favored military expenditures over decent housing and healthcare for the poor. What was one's responsibility in such situations? Even if one were not directly responsible for setting unfair policies, were there not "sins of omission" to be reckoned with if one did not oppose injustices? Compounding confusion were conversations about the primacy of conscience. How was a person to discern its appositeness? What initially seemed like a breath of fresh air was soon recognized as a responsibility to be assumed with profound humility before God about one's decisions and their consequences. Catholics had a lot to deal with as they found sin, conversion, and their sacramental confessions more complicated than they once thought.

While Catholics sorted out legal metaphors associated with the sacrament that no longer seemed relevant, lines for confession lessened. Attendance at Sunday Eucharistic Liturgy remained steady, and in some places grew, but the practice of sacramental confession gradually declined.

Was it time for a new look at the sacrament of penance? The sacrament had experienced permutations before; was a new form, a new ritual, a new approach, due? Bishops and theologians who gathered at the Second Vatican Council (1962–1965) thought so.

The New Rite of Penance

The new Rite of Penance appeared in 1973 with much to commend it as a source to reinvigorate the sacrament.[12]

First, the new rite assumed that sin is a social, as well as a personal, reality and was sensitive to the fact that sins of injustice, poverty, and prejudice undeniably hurt community life. It retained the best from traditional models of church as a community responsible for widows

---

[11] See William Reiser, *Renewing the Baptismal Promises: Their Meaning for the Christian Life* (New York: Pueblo, 1988), 12–13.

[12] *The Rite of Penance* (Washington, DC: United States Catholic Conference, 1973).

and orphans and served as a wake-up call that widows and orphans, as well as many others caught in a net of injustice, were still in need of attention, prayer, advocacy, and hands-on service on their behalf.

The Rite affirmed that there is really no such thing as a private sin. All sins, even those sins committed alone or without witnesses, create a fallout that affects the community. The community is lessened by sin—it is diminished as the community of saints that it is destined to be.

Furthermore, the Rite offered and recommended communal penance services to reinforce the presence and involvement of the community in sin and repentance. Of the three rites available, Rite A represented reconciliation of individual penitents, basically a repetition of the traditional form. Two communal options, Rite B and Rite C, were also available. Rite B gathered the community for prayer, song, and proclamation of Scriptures, included a homily, a general confession of sins along with individual confession and absolution, and a prayer of praise. It served as a hybrid, combining the values of individual and communal penance, as well as an individual and communal sense of sin. It has been said that Pope Paul VI remarked about this rite that "it unites the double merit of community act and personal act. This is the best form for our people when it is possible."[13]

Rite C gathered the community in prayer, song, and the reading of Scripture, but it differed from Rite B since it allowed for *communal* confession of sin and *communal* absolution. Even though Rite C clearly stipulated that penitents guilty of mortal sin were obliged to confess individually at another time,[14] bishops' conferences the world over have been reluctant to grant authorization for this celebration of the sacrament except when emergency circumstances prevail—for example, if an unexpected number of penitents arrive for Rite B, and there are too few confessors available to hear individual confessions. There was, and still is, a perception among some that Rite C is too indulgent, too much a "Protestant" style, and that it allows an easy way out for penitents not willing to face up to their sins. On the other hand, men and women who have been part of such liturgies speak

[13] See Doris Donnelly, "The New Rite of Penance: A Place to Meet God and Neighbor," *Sign*, (April 1976): 22.

[14] *Rite of Penance*, "Introduction," 60.

of them as edifying, moving, and reverent experiences and as visible and palpable expressions of the church as sinful and holy at the same time.

Second, the reformed Rite revisioned the role of priest. "Fervent prayer, prudence, and deep knowledge of God's action in the hearts of people"[15] are identified as prerequisites for this ministry. The Rite also limits a prior emphasis on the confessor's role as judge and replaced that accent with pastoral references: he is, more fittingly, "to reflect the image of Christ the Good Shepherd,"[16] entrusted as he is with extending the merciful ministry of Christ.

The 1973 Rite of Penance intended to restore to the sacrament of penance a sense of its reality as the sign to the whole world of Christ's forgiving love. It approached the revision of rites and formulas in the sacrament with sensitivity to the past, which is, of course, normative for the church, but always in dialogue with the present. The reform emerged, then, not as a change in essentials, but rather as the rediscovery of essentials in a contemporary context.

The Rite did much to reeducate and to revivify stale and sometimes impoverished approaches to sin and conversion. Yet, for all it had going for it, with its pastoral orientation, social consciousness, justice orientation, and communal and liturgical sensitivity, it has not been able to stem the tide of indifference to the sacrament among Catholics. Anecdotal evidence about the lack of interest in the sacrament is supported by research from the Center for Applied Research in the Apostolate (CARA) at Georgetown University, which reports that "three-quarters of Catholics never participate in the sacrament of Reconciliation or that they do so less than once a year."[17] At the same time, a great deal of time and money is spent on counsellors who help expunge guilt from our lives, heal hurtful relationships of the past, and restore peace in the turbulence of our daily routines. Yet the Rite of Penance, now known more familiarly as the sacrament of reconciliation, is infrequently the "go-to" place for words of pardon, wisdom, and encouragement.

[15] Ibid., 10a.

[16] Ibid., 10c.

[17] See the 2008 study http://cara.georgetown.edu/sacramentsreport.pdf, accessed May 14, 2014.

Why is this so? Why do Catholics not seek this sacrament of God's love and mercy to meet the hungers of the human heart? Five reasons come to mind.

First, the sacrament of penance was not—at least for many—a source of spiritual growth. Those old enough to remember weekly and monthly confessions reported to the study that, prior to 1973, penances were regularly prescribed and fulfilled, but there was rarely any dramatic change in the penitents' ethical and spiritual lives afterward. Impatience, lust, greed, jealousy, and indifference still ruled one's life. A practice that did not work was simply abandoned and not missed.

Second, there was unease about penances, the prayers customarily assigned by the priest at the conclusion of sacramental confession. It is not that penitents were looking for more arduous penances, but those prescribed seemed to miss an opportunity to assist in the conversion process. Thomas Kuhlman, a clinical psychologist, notes that unrelated and insignificant penances for serious and significant sins could easily have had the effect of trivializing the sin. Perhaps the sin was not that important or as heinous as one thought if the penance was puny. Perhaps, after all, the sin was puny, too. And perhaps the responsibility in justice of righting the wrong the sin caused might even be dismissed entirely. Kuhlman writes, "When penances are mechanical and easy, going to confession can easily become what psychologists call a 'neutralizing technique'—that is, a way to defuse the negative emotions one experiences as a result of one's actions. . . . The next time one struggles with temptation . . . the consequence of sin that will come to mind may be less the damage it causes to oneself and others than the good feelings the act of going to confession occasions." [18]

Third, continued emphasis on private, individual, integral, auricular confession reinforced the private nature of sin and repentance, thus marginalizing the ecclesial dimension of the sacrament. Without a community context, a social dimension of sin, or an experience of corporate responsibility for sin, one could seek forgiveness from God privately, apart from the official sacramental ministry of the church. It seemed possible to find peace and healing elsewhere. (One won-

---

[18] Thomas L. Kuhlman, "The Floating Sacrament: How We Confess Today," *Commonweal* Magazine (April 6, 2012): 14–15.

ders, if this observation is as pervasive as it seems, whether Rite C deserves a second look.)

Fourth, hypocrisy in the church, its unwillingness to admit sin in its own house, compounded by an attitude of being above the law that binds everyone else, has been a tough pill for Catholics to swallow. At the end of the movie that chronicles her life in a home for pregnant, unmarried young women, Philomena Lee chooses to forgive the nuns who gave away (sold?) her son as punishment for her sins and lied to her and to her son, both of whom wanted contact with each other. Because of the duplicity and sheer callousness of the nuns, mother and son never met. Philomena's act of forgiveness is heroic.[19] Others are no less generous but simply dismayed that a church that preaches repentance is having such a hard time acknowledging its sins and begging forgiveness from those whose lives it has, often enough—too often by most measure—destroyed.

What is most galling to Catholics who reflect on the sexual abuse crisis is that the persons sinned against are virtually ignored, left to fend for themselves. According to Thomas Kuhlman: "A confessional practice that took both justice and psychology more seriously would be more concerned with redressing the real effects of sin, the habits it forms, and the suffering it causes its victims."[20] It is true that the 1973 Rite of Penance clearly directs the confessor in this regard: "If a penitent has been the cause of harm or scandal to others, the priest should lead him to resolve that he will make appropriate restitution."[21] But the Rite's directive, at least in practice, is not the norm. "How few confessors," writes Thomas Kulhman, "insist that we apologize to those our sins have hurt if we haven't already, and try to make amends insofar as that's possible? . . . This is discouraging."[22]

[19] *Philomena*, a film released by the Weinstein Company, directed by Stephen Frears, written by Steve Coogan and Jeff Pope, is based on the book *The Lost Child of Philomena Lee* by Martin Sixsmith. In his *New York Times* review, November 21, 2013, Steven Holden wrote: "A major theme of this film is forgiveness. Ms. Dench's Philomena Lee glows with the radiance of someone serene in her faith despite inhuman treatment by the church. That she makes you believe her character has the capacity to forgive provides the movie with a solid moral center."

[20] Kuhlman, "The Floating Sacrament," 15.

[21] *Rite of Penance*, 18.

[22] Kuhlman, "The Floating Sacrament," 15–16.

Fifth, according to liturgical theologian Joseph Martos, "the single moral issue which probably led more Catholic lay people to question the nature and necessity of confession was not a global one but a personal one: birth control."[23] Although Catholic theologians were undecided about the morality of the contraceptive pill, the church's hierarchy decided it did not qualify as a " 'natural' means of birth control and declared it sinful. . . . [But] many married Catholics," according to Martos, "did not see anything sinful about it. . . . [So] in time, Catholics simply stopped mentioning birth control in the confessional, and the image of the priest as the final arbiter in moral matters began to be discarded."[24] In increasing numbers, married couples made their peace with God without the aid of the sacrament. Simply put, the sacrament did not satisfy their need for assistance with the difficult personal decisions they had to make.

With these concerns, and others, the question that remains is whether it is possible to turn the tide and to have the sacrament of penance, conversion, reconciliation, and repentance move into the mainstream of sacramental life. What are the prospects for the future? Let us see.

Does the Sacrament of Penance Have a Future?

Unburdening is an archetypal need that all psychologically healthy human beings share. It involves a need to divest oneself of what stands in the way of freedom, the need to be released from guilt that paralyzes, the need to confess errors of judgment and pain caused to others, or the need to negotiate pain caused by others to us. All of the major religions of the world respond to this need. Among Catholic Christians, the need is met in a variety of ways. One of those responses has been through the various permutations of what we now call the sacrament of penance.

One would think that the sacrament would be enjoying a heyday in Roman Catholic circles, that people would be queuing up for this spiritual service and sharing information about its availability to others. Here is the possibility not only to confess one's sins but also

---

[23] Martos, *Doors to the Sacred*, 360.
[24] Ibid., 361.

to hear consoling words of forgiveness, to express one's responsibility and sorrow for dreadful deeds done and be met by a promise that sins though scarlet shall be made as white as snow (Isa 1:18). That the sacrament is neglected and considered inconsequential for many Catholics is already documented in these pages. Now is the time to assess what the sacrament of penance might look like in the future and what might help its revival.

I offer four modest trajectories for consideration among those who find the sacrament irrelevant, as encouragement for those willing to give the sacrament another try, and as consolation for those whose affection for the sacrament was never lost in a fog. They all rely on Pope Francis as their source.

Pope Francis has his finger on the pulse of sin; God's mercy, love, and forgiveness; repentance; and the sacrament of penance. There is not a week that goes by when he does not address one or more of these themes. Perhaps the most surprising revelation, because it occurred in a widely reported press interview, was how Pope Francis identified himself. Father Antonio Spadaro,[25] the interviewer, reports: "I ask Pope Francis point-blank: 'Who is Jorge Mario Bergoglio?'[26] He stares at me in silence. I ask him if I may ask him this question. He nods and replies: 'I do not know what might be the most fitting description. . . . I am a sinner. This is the most accurate definition. It is not a figure of speech, a literary genre. I am a sinner.'"[27] The effect of the revelation is: he is one of us. Yes, he is priest, Jesuit, pope, but he admits that he faces temptations as we do, and sometimes fails in living his Christian commitment. He meets the requirements as a bona fide sinner.

What the pope does not say, but which is also true and far more important, is that he is a *forgiven sinner*. We are able to verify this assessment from the parable of the unforgiving debtor (Matt 18:21-35). In that text, the acid test for determining whether a person has

---

[25] Antonio Spadaro, a Jesuit priest, is editor-in-chief of the Italian journal *La Civiltà Cattolica*.

[26] Jorge Mario Bergoglio is Pope Francis's family name.

[27] The text of the interview is available in a variety of venues, among them, the Vatican website: http://www.vatican.va/holy_father/francesco/speeches/2013/september/documents/papa-francesco_20130921_intervista-spadaro_en.html, accessed May 13, 2014.

accepted the forgiveness of God is that he or she is lavish in extending mercy and forgiveness to others. The corollary is also true: the
person stingy in forgiving others is one who has not accepted the
forgiveness of God. Pope Francis is exemplary in lavishing forgiveness and mercy in God's name. Ergo, he must be a forgiven sinner.

The very consoling benefit of acknowledging one's sinfulness and
accepting God's forgiveness is freedom. That gift seems to be abun-
dantly evident in the life of Pope Francis. The pope's persona, his *joie
de vivre*, and his personal freedom qualify as attractive recommenda-
tions to others for the sacrament.

Second, the pope has strengthened guidelines for confessors. For
Pope Francis, the good confessor is "tender and strong" as he gives
witness to new life offered in the sacrament. "This witness," the pope
said in an address in March 2014 to a gathering of the Apostolic
Penitentiary, "is read on the face and heard in the voice of the priest."[28]
The priest must welcome penitents "not with the attitude of a judge
and not like a simple friend, but with the charity of God, with the
love of a father who sees his son returning and then heads his way
(to meet him), like a shepherd who has found a lost sheep." "Confession is not a prosecuting court," he reminded his audience, "but an
experience of forgiveness and mercy."

Pope Francis takes into account that it is not easy to approach the
sacrament. For some people it takes courage, so priests must be in touch
with their own humanity, "so as never to be an obstacle, but always
to be of help drawing others to God's mercy and forgiveness."[29]

By the way, priests who preside at Rite B, the rite that gathers the
community for individual confession and absolution in a communal
setting of prayer and reflection, report that when they begin the celebration with a prayer that positions themselves as sinners along with
everyone else, a greater comfort level is experienced throughout the
congregation. Anything that conveys a "me-as-holy" and "you-as-
sinner" frame of reference is not only off-putting but also diametri-
cally opposed to the proper tone for the sacramental celebration. Pope
Francis addresses precisely that mentality: "Such an attitude poisons
God's merciful grace," he cautions. It often happens, Francis says,

---

[28] "Pope Francis's Address to Apostolic Penitentiary," http://www.zenit.org/en
/articles/pope-francis-address-to-apostolic-penitentiary, accessed May 13, 2014.
[29] Ibid.

"that a person comes and says: 'I haven't been to Confession for many years, I have had this problem, I left going to Confession because I met a priest and he said this to me,' and we see the imprudence, the lack of pastoral love, in what the person says. And they go away, because of a bad experience in their Confession."[30]

Pope Francis is banking heavily on a renewed spirit and commitment from priests for this sacrament. "Where there is fidelity, the fruits are seen." His approach may not disentangle all of the issues connected with the sacrament of penance, but given the reports identified earlier in this essay about the insensitivity of confessors and their lack of human understanding, it certainly is a step in the right direction.

Third, Pope Francis is an especially persuasive campaigner on behalf of God's mercy.

Does it seem inappropriate to suggest that he echoes William Shakespeare's Portia in her famous speech in *The Merchant of Venice*, when she pled for mercy on Shylock's behalf? "The quality of mercy is not strained," she says, and then continues:

[It] droppeth as the gentle rain from heaven
Upon the place beneath: it is twice blest.[31]

Mercy, Portia says, is more important than the king's scepter because that accoutrement only represents earthly power:

[But] mercy is above this sceptred sway;
It is enthroned in the hearts of kings,
It is an attribute to God himself.[32]

Here we have the pope and Portia in total agreement. Pope Francis speaks of mercy as eloquently as she. According to Francis, mercy is "tender," "patient," "does not seek to humiliate,"[33] "and "has a very

[30] Ibid.

[31] *The Merchant of Venice*, Act 4, Scene 1.

[32] Ibid.

[33] Pope Francis, "Regina Cæli, St. Peter's Square, Second Sunday of Easter: Divine Mercy Sunday," April 7, 2013, http://www.vatican.va/holy_father/francesco/angelus/2013/documents/papa-francesco_regina-coeli_20130407_en.html, accessed May 13, 2014.

special capacity for forgetting."[34] "Mercy can restore life to dry bones."[35] And it is available for the asking to make all things new. One medium where this can happen, according to the pope, who not only talked the talk but also walked the walk by celebrating the sacrament in public as a penitent on March 28, 2014, is in the sacrament of penance.

It is Portia again who calls attention to the fact that "the quality of mercy is not strained." No one shows mercy because he or she has to. It is a gift. Because God, by definition, is love, God cannot be limited by our transgressions. God exercises forgiving love as a constant. Whether we accept or decline God's forgiveness and mercy is up for grabs, ours to decide. We have free will to say yes or no to the offer. From God's perspective, it is an offer God hopes we do not refuse.

A fourth and last word on the future of the sacrament of penance has to do with timing. Once again, we turn to Francis, who presided at a celebration of Rite B in St. Peter's Basilica. The celebration took place during Lent 2014, a fitting time, according to liturgists, for the Rite.[36] All things considered, the timing of Lent is optimal. Ash Wednesday sets the background, and forty days is a good chunk of time to do some soul searching in between tax season (a preoccupation in the United States), spring break, and all the other things that fill our schedules.

Pope Francis assures us that God is eager to absorb whatever mistakes, errors of judgment, flaws, imperfections, and sins emerge in the review of our hearts. We can choose to keep them to ourselves, but Francis recommends turning everything over to a merciful Christ who has the power to separate us from our sins as far as the east

[34] "Homily of Pope Francis, Holy Mass in the Parish of St. Anna in the Vatican, Fifth Sunday of Lent, March 17, 2013," http://www.vatican.va/holy_father/francesco/homilies/2013/documents/papa-francesco_20130317_omelia-santa-anna_en.html, accessed May 13, 2014.

[35] "*Urbi et Orbi* Message of Pope Francis, Easter 2013: Easter Sunday, March 13, 2013," http://www.vatican.va/holy_father/francesco/messages/urbi/documents/papa-francesco_20130331_urbi-et-orbi-pasqua_en.html, accessed May 13, 2014.

[36] Ash Wednesday in particular is recommended, as is the Lenten season. See *Rite of Penance*, 37, for reasons why these times might be fitting "to promote conversion of life and purification of heart."

is from the west (Ps 103:12), an expression of infinity, and who is ready to refresh us with words of unending assurances, love, and tenderness.

If the sacrament of penance has a future, a renewed place in the life of Catholic Christians, much will depend on the personal witness of people who can speak from experience about the transformation it effects. One pope, a sinner, has paved the way. Secure in his identity as a forgiven sinner, joyful in the exercise of his ministry, energized to do justice for the neglected, ignored, impoverished among us with kindness and compassion, the benefits of living in the freedom of Christ looks very appealing indeed.

5

Marriage and Justice

Natalie Kertes Weaver

"I thought I was doing all right, that is, until I took this class. Now, I'm not sure." These were words a student shared with me after completing my Theology of Family course. She went on to tell me she was a single mother, having divorced years ago after discovering her husband's infidelity. The act pushed her to divorce, but the marriage itself had been tense and unhappy, even abusive at times. After dealing with the financial struggles of single parenthood for nearly a decade, this student decided she might improve her lot if she returned to college. She had a live-in boyfriend but no intention of marrying again. Her focus had shifted to her own career development. Now, in light of her study, she felt judged by the church. Was she inadequate as a parent because she was divorced? Was she immoral in her lifestyle choice because, although she did not want to be alone, she now valued self-sufficiency more than marriage? The incident was a powerful reminder for me as a Catholic theologian teaching family and marriage. The people I encounter, perhaps more often than not, have family lives and personal experiences that differ profoundly from the ideal conception of sacramental marriage as it is understood and taught by the Catholic Church.

The Catholic Church teaches that marriage is a sacrament, a sacred mystery, a physical sign of God's invisible grace.[1] When born of the legal and free consent of the man and woman as witnessed in the eyes of the church, and subsequently consummated through sexual intercourse, the church teaches that marriage becomes an indissoluble union. Just as Christ and the church exist in permanent, covenantal relationship to one another, Christian marriage constitutes a permanent relationship between a baptized man and a baptized woman. The Christian marital relationship does not simply mirror the boundless love between Christ and the church. It is a graced instantiation of that sacred dynamic. Christian married couples comprise a significant population of the church. Stated more plainly, to a large extent, married couples *are* the church. Therefore, as married persons and in the context of their family lives, men and women actively participate in the creative, healing, and salvific work of the church. Marriage becomes a microcosm of the universal church and is thus imbued with the grace of the church, along with the character and responsibilities that flow from that grace.

This sacramental theology of marriage is a perennially beautiful and hopeful conception of what marriages can aspire to be. And yet, marriages in their lived-in realities often feel quite different and fall quite short of these noble aspirations. This is all the more true when we broaden our discussion to include sex and reproduction, which, according to the theological tradition, belong within the context of sacramental marriage but, in reality, often extend well beyond the moral parameters for sex that the church teaches. It is illustrative to acknowledge some of these differences, especially as they surface in today's classrooms.[2] Some students have children already, and often

---

[1] Consult the *Code of Canon Law* (Vatican City/Washington, DC: Libreria Editrice Vaticana/Canon Law Society of America, 1989), 1055–1165.

[2] The Guttmacher Institute, a premier research institute on sex and reproductive health, reports that by age nineteen, seven of ten males and females have had sexual intercourse, with over 80 percent using condoms or oral contraceptives or both at the time of first intercourse. While the average age at first sexual intercourse is seventeen, the average age at the time of marriage is in the mid-twenties. Ninety percent of teens who do not use contraceptives become pregnant within a year of first sexual intercourse. In a 2002 survey, 3 percent of males and 8 percent of females reported a homosexual or bisexual orientation. Close to 200,000 abortions occurred in 2008 in women fifteen to nineteen years old, most of whom reported that they either could

those children are born outside the context of marriage. Young people today are commonly sexually active before marriage, frequently with multiple partners (either serially or simultaneously). While between 60 and 70 percent of American and European teenagers are sexually active, evidence suggests that 90 percent of students are sexually active by their senior year of college, even though they are unlikely to marry until their mid-twenties.[3] Related to this datum, many use birth control. Some are cohabiting. Many others will cohabit with an intimate partner before marriage. Some are homosexual, and among homosexual students, one finds varying levels of self-understanding and self-acceptance. Some students report having survived intimate-partner violence situations. Some are adopted. Some have experience living in foster homes. Many come from divorced, blended, or single-parent households.[4]

At the beginning of each term, I ask students to discuss their perceptions of contemporary family life, whether they think of marriage as a religious institution, and what factors influence their understanding of marriage. Every term, students say they do not think of marriage as foremost a religious institution. They think of it as a personal matter that involves the church only peripherally. For those students planning a wedding, mention of coordinating with the church or finding a priest to celebrate the wedding can elicit a flood of contentious commentary. "Why does the priest ask so many questions?" "He wants us to live apart before the wedding." "What's with the compatibility test they make us take?" "They won't marry us outside, and we wanted to have an outdoor wedding ceremony."

Anyone equipped with a computer, phone, or television today has been exposed to hypersexual audio and visual stimulation from childhood. All have been bombarded with consumer-oriented images of marriage (ranging from the sale of diamonds, travel, furnishings,

---

not afford or were not mature enough to rear a child. For full data and research articles on American teens' sex and reproductive health issues, please consult www.guttmacher.org.

[3] See Jan E. Palmer, MD, "Birth Control Counseling Opportunities: The Freshman Naïveté," *American Journal of Health Studies* 20 (2005): 47–57.

[4] Annual statistical information on marriage and divorce events in the United States is collected by the United States Census Bureau. Their complete, public reports may be accessed at www.census.gov.

insurance, and even pharmaceuticals). From television programming, such as ABC's *The Bachelor* or TLC's *Say Yes to the Dress*, to wedding expos at major convention centers throughout the country, marriage is portrayed as socially desirable but largely devoid of deep religious meaning.

Contemporary, popular attitudes toward sex, gender, and relationship roles further compound conceptions of marriage shaped by family history and popular media. Classical models of marriage have been transforming for decades.[5] In traditional societies, marriage was contracted for the legitimate reproduction of children and the joining of individuals and families for mutual economic prosperity (and in marginalized societies, the more fundamental goal of basic economic survival). Today, a desire for family and financial stability may be contributing factors to a couple's decision to wed, but they are often secondary to egoistic pursuits of love, happiness, and pleasure.[6] Marriage undertaken for personal love and happiness may be significantly at odds with marriage undertaken as a duty to community, extended family, and society at large. In light of a pervasive culture of individualism in modern consumer-based societies, women and men often delay marriage in the interests of education and career development. And, as especially women (in Western contexts) have become more financially independent, marriage has become an option for life and family rather than a necessity.[7]

Against this backdrop, the Catholic teaching on marriage as a sacrament can be interpreted as everything from prophetic revelation to antiquated ideal to unrealistic expectation to even foolish optimism. Moreover, as my student's opening comments suggest, this teaching can even seem condemnatory of the average person's life

---

[5] For a discussion of the historical transformation of marriage from ecclesiastical to contractual models, consult John Witte, Jr., *From Sacrament to Contract: Marriage, Religion, and Law in Western Tradition* (Louisville, KY: Westminster John Knox Press, 1997).

[6] Stephanie Coontz explores the historical development of marriage from an institution of necessity to one undertaken for personal satisfaction and happiness in her work *Marriage, a History: From Obedience to Intimacy or How Love Conquered Marriage* (New York: Viking Penguin, 2005).

[7] For a discussion of the changing face of marriage today, see Andrew J. Cherlin's *The Marriage-Go-Round: The State of Marriage and the Family in America Today* (New York: Vintage, 2010).

circumstances, fraught as they are with the disappointments and shortcomings that complicate even the best laid plans. After all, most people do not marry with the intent to divorce; yet nearly half of all marriages fail.[8]

The justice issues that pertain to marriage as a sacrament, then, must be viewed in light of the contextual reality of marriage and family life. Ever shifting, this context includes everything that conditions and frames experience, such as geopolitics, history, economics, technological developments, education, workforce instability, and so on. As contexts change, so do the justice questions pertaining to the teaching that marriage is a sacrament. In this sense, the questions of marriage and justice cannot be seen in a linear, developmental perspective; the church's teaching has not consistently, diachronically improved the condition of married persons or their state in society from previous ages to the present one. Rather, basic justice questions surface in every context, and within all contexts. The church's teaching intersects with people's lives in contextually determined ways. In one era or geographic location, the church's teaching may resonate as liberating and revelatory; in another, as stifling and even problematic.[9]

The justice questions must further be construed in three additional relational categories experienced by married persons and their families.[10] First, the church's teaching may be seen as most immediately affecting the married couple itself. Church teaching, for example, about

[8] A fascinating survey of the legal and ideological representations of divorce in America from the country's origins until the modern-day era of no-fault divorce is found in Norma Basch's *Framing American Divorce: From the Revolutionary Generation to the Victorians* (Berkeley and Los Angeles: University of California Press, 2001).

[9] Rosemary Radford Ruether speaks poignantly of this point in her work *Disputed Questions on Being a Christian* (Maryknoll, NY: Orbis Books, 1989). In Ruether's discussion of her emergence into feminism, she comments on the distinction between (1) women who have reproductive freedom and thus can process the church's teaching on contraception through the filter of conscience, and (2) women who lack reproductive freedom or lack the social context in which it is possible for them freely either to embrace or reject the church's teaching for their own safety and welfare. In the absence of opportunities for conscientious objection, the church's teaching on marriage and family can effectively enslave women to marriage and childbearing.

[10] Michael Lawler helpfully explains these relationships in the language of marriage "bonds." As Lawler describes, marriage has natural, civil, and ecclesial bonds, each of which has elements that both strengthen and also obligate the married couple in

the essentially procreative end of sex and the correlated prohibition of artificial contraception most immediately affects the married couple, for they will be responsible for the children they bear. The church's teaching on the permanence of marriage also binds the husband and wife for the entirety of their lives, yet it is the individual man and woman who must consequently live out the challenge of that permanence. From one social location to the next, the degree of freedom and personal expression one experiences in the roles of husband and wife, as well as what each can anticipate from the other as spouses, varies. Along with this varied experience arises conflicting received experiences of the church's teaching on marital indissolubility.

The second relational category is that of marriage in society. Here, one considers questions about the statutes and laws of the polis concerning marriage and family life. For example, laws that restrict marriage or divorce, as well as laws that prescribe or proscribe birth control and regulate childbirth contextually define marriage. It is important to acknowledge that marriage both preexisted the Christian era and occurs in all cultural and religious contexts. A sacramental theology of marriage, then, is a lens through which to interpret the meaning of marriage; however, marriage can and does occur independently of that lens. Just as Catholic married persons are a constitutive part of the church, so also are they a constitutive part of the societies in which they exist. The state has a stake in interpreting and shaping marriage, which may complement or even conflict with the church's lens. In addition, the family, as a family and as a unit of the state, has certain obligations to the state and thus must consider justice issues related to the family's commitment to the commonweal.[11]

The third relationship is that which exists between the married family unit and the church. The church defines the marriages of its faithful as an integral part of its sacramental life. Church teaching establishes the basic framework for instruction about good marriage, licit sexual conduct, and family life. In this regard, the church sets

---

their commitment. Consult his text *Marriage and the Catholic Church: Disputed Questions* (Collegeville, MN: Liturgical Press, 2002).

[11] Lisa Sowle Cahill argues this point well in her work *Family: A Christian Social Perspective* (Minneapolis, MN: Augsburg Fortress Press, 2000).

forth its benchmarks and also its expectations for married people. But the church also has an obligation to support and bolster married people and their families. In its teachings, its social services, its educational opportunities for children, and more, the church is challenged to strengthen its ministers in the sacrament of marriage. Surveying the historical church, one sees varying achievements in this regard.

Bearing in mind the personal, civil, and ecclesial dimensions of marriage in context, consider two major moments in the history of Christian marriage: (1) before it was a sacrament, and (2) after it was a sacrament. Such a consideration illustrates the contextual nature of the questions of justice in marriage and sets the stage for considering that question today.

Marriage was not always recognized as a sacrament. For over one thousand years, the Catholic Church was undecided about the status of marriage. On the one hand, the Bible supported the belief that God had created the human couple for marriage. The opening chapter of Genesis describes God's creation of the heavens and earth, the plants and the animals. After the perfect stage is set, God brings forth the crowning achievement of creation, namely, the human couple:

> God created humankind in his image, in the image of God he created them; male and female he created them. God blessed them, and God said to them, "Be fruitful and multiply, and fill the earth and subdue it; and have dominion over the fish of the sea and over the birds of the air and over every living thing that moves upon the earth." (Gen 1:27-28)

In the above passage, the singleness of the human couple in creation is stressed; in the second chapter of Genesis, the bond of companionship stands out. In this telling of creation, God first makes Adam. Judging that it is not good for Adam to be alone, God brings forth all the animals and presents them to Adam. To each, Adam gives a name, but no animal proves to be a suitable companion. It is then that God creates the man's partner from his own rib.

> So the Lord God caused a deep sleep to fall upon the man, and he slept; then he took one of his ribs, and closed up its place with flesh. And the rib that the Lord God had taken from the man he made into a woman and brought her to the man. Then the man said, "This at last is bone of my bones and flesh of my flesh; this one shall be called

Woman, for out of Man this one was taken." Therefore a man leaves
his father and his mother and clings to his wife, and they become
one flesh. (Gen 2:21)

Derived from the Hebrew biblical tradition, the doctrine of creation
in Christian theology justifies the claim that marriage is God's original
plan for human life. Moreover, the biblically stated goal of marriage
is procreation, as God instructs the couple to "go forth, and multiply."
That God created marriage and human sexuality seemed to the Christian community of the first millennium a powerful endorsement of
the good of marriage. This endorsement was further bolstered by the
scriptural motif of using marriage as a metaphor to describe the relationship between God and humankind. The Israelites in the Old
Testament[12] frequently described the people as bound to God in a
covenantal relationship that was as intimate and permanent as human
marriage. The Christians of the New Testament[13] borrowed this metaphor and applied it liberally to Jesus and the church. The language
of bride (church) and bridegroom (Christ) became powerful words
in describing Jesus' connection to his community of believers.

Given this high estimation of marriage and reproductive sexuality,
it is perhaps confusing that Christians of this era were not convinced
that marriage was a sacred thing. Traditions regarding marriage,
family, and sexuality in the first millennium were multilayered and
had intermingled theological and cultural aspects. The cultural aspects
can be summarized as reflecting the widespread patriarchal customs
and social structures of the Mediterranean peoples. The Hebrew,
Greek, and Roman backdrops of early Christianity were cultures in
which men played a predominate role in family and political spheres.
Women and children were valued for their contributions to the family,
especially economically, but they were not afforded status as social
equals to men.[14] This reflected the prevailing attitude that women
were inferior to men existentially, physically, intellectually, morally,

---

[12] See, for example, Hosea and Song of Songs.

[13] See, for example, Ephesians.

[14] Consult Bonnie Maclachlan, *Women in Ancient Greece: A Sourcebook* (New York:
Continuum, 2012); Beryl Rawson, *Marriage, Divorce, and Children in Ancient Rome*
(Oxford and New York: Oxford University Press, 1991); and T. M. Lemos, *Marriage
Gifts and Social Change in Ancient Palestine: 1200 BCE to 200 CE* (New York: Cambridge
University Press, 2010).

and volitionally. Among the Greeks especially, whose philosophical framework established the principal context for Christian doctrinal development in the patristic era, women were associated with body and nature while men were associated with mind and spirit.[15] This association became particularly problematic in the Christian era, as the body was blamed for the weakness in humans that led to sin. The Gospel of Matthew, for example, relates Jesus encouraging his disciples to pray lest they fall into temptation because "the spirit indeed is willing, but the flesh is weak" (Matt 26:41).

Bodily sin, moreover, was interpreted in a particularly sexual light, so that sexual desire, pleasure, and conjugal love were viewed as the seat of human corruption. Taken to its extreme, early Christian commentators actually viewed sexual intercourse as the means by which original sin was transmitted, akin to infectious disease. Thus, although God had created sex for the purpose of procreation, it had become disfigured in the fall in the Garden of Eden. Thereafter, all sex was tainted by the stain of sin and lust.

Compounding the general mistrust over the sexual body was the overriding issue of salvation for early Christians. Jesus' life had ended in the horrible death of the crucifixion. While Christians could attempt to live worthy and faith-filled lives, their ultimate goal shifted to hope for a final resurrection, anticipated in Jesus' resurrection, and the full coming of the reign of God. Jesus' life and death had initiated the Christian era, but Christians awaited his Second Coming in order to see their hopes fulfilled. Life on this earth, then, and concerns for the normal aspects of living (such as acquisition of material wealth, marriage, and family life) were suborned to preparation of the spirit for eternal life. It was esteemed more valuable to live a celibate life in service to God than to marry, that is, if one could avoid marriage.[16] Thus was born the distinction in Christianity between (1) the superior, celibate class of ordained men and vowed religious women and (2) the lesser class of married men and women.

---

[15] See the discussion of Greek philosophical frameworks in Nancy Tuana's *Woman and the History of Philosophy* (St. Paul, MN: Paragon House, 1998).

[16] See Paul's teaching in 1 Cor 7:1-9.

In this theological and cultural climate, Christianity developed a split mind on marriage and sexuality.[17] It was God's creation but tainted by sin. It was necessary for the birth of children but spiritually distracting. This split attitude can be seen, for example, in St. Augustine's (354–430) mixed commentary on marriage. He argued that marriage was a *sacramentum*, a sacred mystery that reflected the relationship between Christ and the church. Yet he also maintained that sex was inherently lustful and that marriage merely provided boundaries for the proper direction of lustful urges and the lawful production of children.[18] While Augustine early anticipated that the church would eventually define marriage as a sacrament, his ambivalent attitude toward marriage reflects a tension in the Christian mind-set that persists even in the present.

The gradual acknowledgment of marriage as a sacrament occurred during a time when the church was rising to prominence in the affairs of daily life. Priests and presbyters were often turned to as arbiters in disputed matters regarding marriage. As a result, it became customary in the Middle Ages for people to post announcements of forthcoming weddings and to conduct the wedding itself in a public location, usually the steps of the church. Wedding ceremonies moved into the church itself, and the priest began to officiate the ceremony, rather than merely bless the couple at the conclusion of an exchange of vows.[19]

The move toward an ecclesial form reflected improvements in the core justice concerns of medieval people intending to marry. The

---

[17] Rosemary Radford Ruether discusses the ambivalent Christian attitude toward bodies and nature, on which the ambivalence about marriage rested, in her work *Gaia and God: An Ecofeminist Theology of Earth Healing* (New York: HarperCollins, 1992), 15–31. Ruether also traces Christian ambivalence toward women in *Women and Redemption: A Theological History* (Minneapolis, MN: Augsburg Fortress Press, 1998).

[18] Augustine's treatise *On the Good of Marriage* exemplifies this mixed attitude, arguing on the one hand that marriage is an indissoluble sacred bond analogous to Christ and the church and on the other that married people are helplessly lustful. For Augustine, the institution of marriage is separable from married people with the former being honorable and the latter debased.

[19] For a detailed discussion of this history, see "Part One: Marriage in Historical Perspective" in *Perspectives on Marriage: A Reader*, ed. Kieran Scott and Michael Warren (New York and Oxford: Oxford University Press, 2001), 7–46.

customs of private marriage, marriage that occurred during inter-course or marriage that was binding at the time of betrothal left people vulnerable to a variety of dilemmas. One betrothed might honor the promise to marry, while another would forsake that promise and enter into a clandestine marriage. One might believe she had wed a man, entering into a sexual union with him, only to learn he was otherwise promised or committed. Perhaps the greatest transgression of justice prior to the establishment of an ecclesial form was the fact that children could be forced to wed by the decisions of their parents.

In light of these particulars, thinkers such as Francis Gratian (ca. 1140) argued for a proper form and formula to marriage. Combining various traditions of betrothal and intercourse as binding aspects of marriage, this canon lawyer argued that a legal and binding marriage would have to be *ratum* (ratified by the free consent of the spouses) and *consummatum* (consummated through sexual intercourse). If a marriage between two baptized Christians was contracted before the witnesses of the church, entered into on the basis of the freely given consent of the spouses, and consummated thereafter, a permanent and sacramental marriage had been entered into, which thereafter would be considered indissoluble by any human act.[20] Marriage was named a sacrament at the Council of Florence (1439). A century later at the Council of Trent (1545–1563), marriage was defined as one of the seven sacraments that Christ instituted for the church, against the Reformers' rejection of a sacramental theology of marriage. Cer-tainly the greatest achievement of sacramental marriage was the condition that marriage could not occur unless by the free consent of the spouses. This marked tremendous improvement in the justice quality of married life insofar as people could not be overtly coerced into marriage against their will.

With the development of a civil or legal dimension to marriage in the early nineteenth century under the Napoleonic Code (1804), the legally positive, socially constructed nature and meaning of marriage

---

[20] The translated text of Gratian's marriage canons is available at http://faculty .cua.edu/Pennington/Canon%20Law/marriagelaw.htm, accessed May 13, 2014. Also see Anders Winroth, *The Making of Gratian's Decretum* (Cambridge and New York: Cambridge University Press, 2000).

came into focus. From the birth of modern nation-states to the present day, civil definitions of and legislation about marriage have extended far beyond the sphere of the church's authority. Dramatic transformations in industry, economy, science, and education from the nineteenth century through the opening decades of the twenty-first century make marriage and family life look today like never before. While the contextual changes are too vast to explore in this venue, it is possible to consider some of the justice concerns that continue to emerge for today's married people vis-à-vis the Catholic theology of marriage. These issues, attached to the relational categories considered earlier, include (1) the need for ongoing improvement in fairness in marriage between men and women, (2) the status of the voice of married people in the church, and (3) lessons from marriage in society today and developing notions of the human.

The Need for Ongoing Improvement in Fairness in Marriage between Men and Women

Interpersonal relationships between men and women have been undergoing transitions for decades. Much has been written on the notion of companionship marriage. The idea that marriage is expressly for the production of children has been replaced by the idea that marriage is foremost for the companionship and unity of spouses. In light of the notion of companionship as a sufficient basis for marriage, new, more egalitarian relationships are today possible, while previous models of hierarchical, and specifically patriarchal, relationships have come under scrutiny. And yet, the legacy of hierarchical, patriarchal marriage persists and even finds modern-day advocates.

Even after marriage was recognized as a sacrament, the church continued to define marriage on the basis of its form in the church, its origin in consent, and its permanence in having been consummated. While the discussion of marriage in canon law does include references to partnership,[21] they occur within the context of the conjugal duty and obligation to procreative sexual intent. Although perhaps implicit in the teaching that marriage is like the relationship

---

[21] See the *Code of Canon Law* (Vatican City/Washington, DC: Libreria Editrice Vaticana/Canon Law Society of America, 1989), 1055; 1063; 1096.

between Christ and the church, there is no explicit instruction in the canonical definition or explanation of permanent sacramental union that spouses must treat each other as equals, do no physical harm to one another, and avoid all manner of abuse.[22]

The exclusion of women from leadership and clerical roles within the church results in, among other things, the absence of women's voices in any authoritative, ecclesial capacity regarding their experiences of marriage. This silencing and theological erasure of women's experiences has historically both produced and reinforced patriarchal ideologies of male and female, of husband and wife. Since the Second Vatican Council, the unitive and procreative ends of marriage have been upheld as coequal, and a new emphasis on mutuality in marriage has surfaced (see GS 47–52). However, the church here and elsewhere teaches "complementarity" between the sexes[23] and makes distinctions between natural, essential roles for men and women within marriage and family life. This model continues to allow for, if not encourage, a patriarchal hierarchy in marriage that mirrors the church's patriarchal hierarchy.

Both the ecclesial and marital hierarchical relationships mutually reinforce male dominance models in society at large. Not only is this ideologically troubling, but the effect of this thinking is borne out in concrete and painful realities for women: the slow move toward women's political enfranchisement, the ongoing vulnerability to physical violence in marriage,[24] the ongoing reality of sexual violence, women's historic exclusion from theological education, and slow access to educational and professional activities until the most recent decades of recorded human history.[25] These power dynamics create

[22] Furthermore, there is at least one curious distinction made between males and females, pertaining to the condition of age at the time of marriage. Canon 1083 considers the licit age for a male at the time of marriage to be sixteen, whereas females can enter into a valid marriage at the age of fourteen. While stated, there is no explanation or justification for this distinction.

[23] Here consult Ivy A. Helman, *Women and the Vatican: An Exploration of Official Documents* (Maryknoll, NY: Orbis, 2012), 48, 54.

[24] Find the United States Department of Justice statistics on intimate partner violence at bjs.ojp.usdoj.gov. Annual reports continue to reveal that nearly one in four women is a victim of intimate partner violence.

[25] Rosemary Radford Ruether critically evaluates the legacy effects of patriarchal marriage in her work *Christianity and the Making of the Modern Family* (Boston: Beacon Press, 2000).

a context of inequity and depersonalization that distort the person-hood of men and women and preclude the emergence of true com-munion.[26] To the extent that women were, and in some cases continue to be, infantilized or deemed morally and intellectually inferior to men, the sacrament of marriage has and will continue to fall short of the full potential of its graced character.

The Status of the Voice of Married People in the Church and Society

The justice question of marriage in relationship to the church hinges on the issue of voice. Married people have had limited voice in the church. In the first millennium of Christianity, during which time major doctrines, creeds, and leadership models of the church were established, marriage was not considered a sacrament. Celibate spirituality defined the highest goal for Christian life. Eastern Ortho-dox and Roman Catholic priests could marry and even take concu-bines in the first millennium, but in the twelfth century, Latin priests and bishops were required by conciliar degree to remain celibate. From that time onward, married persons, men and women, were omitted from the classes of church authority that held highest offices, voted in council, formulated statements of faith, and elected popes.

Beyond the debated justice question of restricting married people from the priesthood and from holding church office, a deeper justice issue concerns the omission of married life as an experiential lens through which Catholic faith is officially focused, articulated, and ultimately held accountable. The overwhelming majority of Catholic persons throughout church history have married rather than lived as celibates, vowed religious, or clerics. Yet, for two thousand years, the natural experiences of human sexual love, fecundity, and com-panionship in the context of married life have been extrinsically defined by those whose theology of marriage, parenthood, and con-jugal sexuality derives from no licit firsthand knowledge. What emerges from this theological model is a condition in which marriage is explained in a formal, ideological, and essential way. It is described in the categories of origin and *telos*, purpose and role-play. But the lived experience and, more important, the ministers of that lived

---

[26] Also see the discussion of this distortion effect in Christine Gudorf, "Western Religion and the Patriarchal Family," in *Perspectives on Marriage*, 285–304.

experience (namely, husbands and wives), are not afforded opportunity to comment in a definitive way on the adequacy of the church's categorical descriptions.[27] Herein lies a critical disconnect between the ideal and the reality of marriage.

As the opening comments of this chapter suggest, a disconnected theology of family and marriage can become either (1) punitive to married people struggling in real time with the challenges of marriage and family life, or (2) incoherent to those who merely reject it as unrealistic, senseless, or passé. In order to stave off this disconnect, the church has an obligation to teach its theology of marriage primarily toward the aim of pastoral care and secondarily toward the aim of orthodoxy. This is especially the case in the church's teaching on annulment and pastoral care of divorced persons. The sacramental theology of marriage teaches that marriage is both an occasion and also a cause of grace, but often the reality of marriage fails to live up to eschatological promise of indissoluble, graced union. When marriages are not successful, the foremost concern of pastors ought to be care of people who are hurting and in need. Too often, divorced and remarried Catholics experience feelings of guilt, shame, and inadequacy that separate them from the church rather than allow them to find the reconciliation and restoration of hope that the church offers.

---

[27] An example of this may be seen in Canons 1151–55, which discuss separation of spouses while the marital bond remains intact (that is, having not been declared null). The circumstances that are noted as cause for separation are adultery and grave mental or physical danger. In the event of adultery, the innocent spouse is required to enter a cause for separation with the proper ecclesiastical authority within six months of learning of the adultery, in order that the church's ministers may work with the innocent spouse to find forgiveness and to stave off separation. If the innocent spouse does not thus involve the church or has conjugal relations with the wayward spouse, the innocent is said to have tacitly condoned the adultery. In any case, once the cause of separation is ended, the spouses are required to live together again. And, once the innocent spouse readmits the offending spouse to conjugal life, the innocent spouse thereafter renounces the right to separate. What is curious about this teaching is that it seems to be ignorant of the broad spectrum effects of living in an abusive or adulterous relationship. It can take years to understand and process the experiences of abuse and infidelity. It can take even more time to overcome feelings of shame and confusion over the heartbreak these experiences raise. In the case of domestic violence, victims often experience limited access to means and avenues of escape. The formal instruction on separation does not reflect pastoral knowledge of the logistical and emotional complexities of responding to abuse and infidelity.

When the voices of the faithful, imperfect as they may be, are included compassionately in the dialogue, the church has the opportunity to grow richer in its wisdom and more effective in its praxis. Drawing from my own experience as a teacher of Catholic theology, I must assume that my senior year students at a Catholic university may have had sex, may use birth control, and may even be cohabiting with a sexual intimate. I am better to honor their personal trajectories as human beings, meeting them where they are, than to speak top-down from the authority of tradition about what their trajectories ought to have been. It is only in entering into the realm of lived experience that the church's teaching can edify, transform, and uplift.

Lessons from Marriage in Society Today and Developing Notions of the Human

More is known today about the human mind, the sexual body, reproductive health, and social organization than ever before. This developing awareness of the human person, based on new sciences situated in modern society, is historically unprecedented. Not only is more known but knowledge is widely diffused throughout all social strata. In this context, modern identity and modern relationships are evolving. It is, I think, premature to speak in conclusive ways about the future state of marriage in light of these developments. However, places to start the conversation acknowledge the experiences of both men and women: freer sex, redefined gender roles, unparalleled personal potential, longer lifespan, economic freedom, better education, etc. This is not to suggest that all of these developments are inherently good. It is to say, rather, that these developments are constitutive elements of the modern experience. The horse is out of the gate, so to speak, on the modern self. Even committed people of faith exist in a liminal state between changing social realities and classical ecclesial teachings.

In the present day, for example, we bear witness to the extraordinary degree to which the state can define marriage, against the authority of the church, in the hotly debated question of legal same-sex marriage. While in some countries, homosexual activity is a capital crime, in other places (as in Europe and North America), gay couples may now legally wed. The issue is among the most politically divisive questions of the day. Both sides of the debate have deeply held convictions regarding civil rights, human nature, personal freedom, biblical teaching, marriage history, and ecclesial authority. The advent of same-sex marriage as a civil reality illustrates poignantly the malleable historical character of marriage.

As new models of family emerge, the absolute power distribution in gender roles (male and female) and hierarchical order (male, female, parental, and sibling) has been irresolutely disrupted. People are today left to craft families, adequate to their needs and desires, yet unmoored from tradition and, worse, from a fundamental culture of responsibility. In affluent nations, moreover, an ethos of consumerism and individualism underlies the struggle of the modern family. Married persons find themselves overworked, overspent, overconsumed, and overmedicated *individuals* trying to live as families but filled with often unrealizable expectations for the self as a *self-within-family*.

The challenges of contemporary family life ripple throughout the whole of the church. For, the church is not Other than but rather instantiated by contemporary families. Contemporary families, put otherwise, are the church and cannot merely be "talked to" or instructed passively by either past voices in the tradition or present-day leadership that wrongly understands itself to be more church than the unruly families it would corral. It is these contemporary families who produce, rear, encourage, or dissuade new ministers, both lay and ordained. It is they who bear and educate the generations of children now and to come. It is they who fill or vacate the pews where they sat as children. It is they who staff, fund, or defund the ministries of the aging religious congregations. It is they who live, transform, transmit, or reject the traditions of their parents and grandparents. In this sense, then, it is fair to say not only that the modern family is in transition but also that the church itself is in transition.

The church's teachings about marriage, then, are received by people who are historically situated and conditioned. The church itself is not an ahistorical entity but rather a living body comprised of living, historically constituted people. While the living body of faithful Catholics receives a tradition that extends backward in time, the members of that body nevertheless receive tradition as persons whose contextual assumptions and worldviews reflect their present day life situation. For the church's teachings to connect with people effectively, its representatives must speak intelligibly within the framework that has made possible modern self-understanding. The church is thus challenged to form and communicate its teachings in contextually sensitive and pastorally oriented ways.

Today, I would suggest that the greatest challenge of the church in all matters of its teaching about marriage and sexuality lies in its willingness to attend anew to the full spectrum of scientific knowledge and discovery about the human person, including all advances in the study of human sexuality and human psychology. In short, the church needs to develop a contemporary theological anthropology that speaks meaningfully in context to the needs of the day. So many of the church's struggles pivot on this point: the role of women in the church, the possibility of married clergy, sexual behavior within and outside of marriage, the questions of sexuality and gender, the sexual continence of the clergy, and more. As modern questions arise, the church will find its best responses in an engaged, vital, and inclusive dialogue that not only teaches what human experience should be but also learns from what human experience has been. It is in this manner that the church's elegant vision of grace-filled, dignified, permanent companionship in marriage and family life can be renewed as a living goal and saved from irrelevance as a static ideal.

The purpose of the church is not to yield to trends, nor is it the church's purpose to bow to error; it is, rather, the church's purpose to proclaim the Gospel of Jesus Christ. In these changing times, one must carefully ask how much that Gospel is actually about the forms, structures, and chronologies of family formation and sexual practice (as has been the default assumption of much church teaching) as opposed to other considerations about how the Gospel might inspire and vivify people within family life.

Perhaps today a just theology of marriage will comment less about when and with whom to have sexual congress and more about inherent personal value and dignity in all sexual persons. I see a just theology of marriage as inviting less instruction about the indissolubility of sacramental marriage and more instruction about the deformities of modern individualism, consumerism, and material irresponsibility that are the roots of spousal unhappiness, parental hardship, and marital decline. I see, moreover, a related theological critique of economic and class privilege that often is reinforced by socially and ecclesially disconnected constructions of family. Modern persons, in addition, are profoundly disfigured by and aware of the patriarchal privilege that disempowers women and makes them globally vulnerable to every manner of exploitation, violence, and abuse. A just theology of marriage will articulate and honestly disclose the church's own historical complicity in creating disfigured relationships through its multi-millennial androcentric legacy of teaching and acting as though women incompletely image God. Finally, a just theology of marriage will occur by and for persons placed within our contemporary situations, so that we are not forced irrationally to create dichotomous epistemologies of faith and science. A just contemporary theology of marriage will be dialogical with and pastorally responsive to the sociopolitical and biomedical sciences that have helped craft the collective modern consciousness in all its complex self-understanding.

Orders and Justice

Thomas J. Scirghi, SJ

In the Italian region of Romagna, they make a special kind of pasta called *Strozzapreti*. They have been making this pasta for centuries. It is made simply with flour, salt, and water, but no eggs, usually a main ingredient for pasta. According to one legend, in the middle of the eighth century, the people of Romagna lived under papal rule and were quite poor. Only a few owned animals and they could not afford eggs, so they developed this simple pasta. Meanwhile, up on the hilltop lived the priests of the town to whom the people paid rent for their land. And the priests lived well, eating meat and fresh vegetables, and they had eggs for making pasta. Because of this, a feeling of anticlericalism developed. The people went about their daily life and continued to make their own simple pasta, which they called *Strozzopreti*, meaning "strangle the priest."

Justice is concerned with right relationships. So when we discuss the link between justice and the sacrament of orders, we need to consider where the ordained ministers—bishops, priests, and deacons—stand in relation to the community of the church.

This right relationship between the ordained minister and the assembly is expressed in the preface to the eucharistic prayer—in the third line of the dialogue between the priest and the congregation. The priest calls out "Let us give thanks to the Lord our God," and the people respond "It is right and just."

The dialogue resembles the "call and response" we often hear in African American churches, when the congregation responds to the preacher with shouts of "Amen." This is no simple emotional outburst; it is a signal of communal affirmation. That is to say, the people are listening attentively and they approve of the sermon thus far. Their shouts encourage the preacher to continue. In this manner, the congregation contributes to the preaching; their participation helps draw out the sermon from the preacher.

In more conventional venues, the congregation prays the prayer with the priest. The three-part dialogue announces what we are about to do as we lift our praise of God in communion with the saints. This is our duty to God—our *leitourgia*, or "liturgy." The priest leads and the people follow, having voiced their support for this call to prayer by announcing, "It is right and just." Here, in a brief interaction, we catch a glimpse of the right relationship between priest and assembly, namely, that the priest is called from within the community to be a spiritual leader for the people of God.

We also hear an echo here of the Rite of Ordination. Candidates for ordination are asked to declare their intentions before the people of God; in turn the people are asked to express their approval. When ordaining a man to the priesthood, a priest or deacon presents the candidate to the bishop, and the bishop asks "Do you know them to be worthy?" The presenter replies, "After inquiry among the Christian people and upon the recommendation of those responsible, I testify that they have been found worthy."[1] We hear a similar statement within the ordination of a bishop. The ordaining bishop states, "The ancient rule of the holy Fathers ordains that a Bishop-elect is to be questioned in the presence of the people on his resolve to uphold the faith and to discharge his duty."[2] The ordination ritual explains where the ordained minister stands in relation to the people of God, the flock of Jesus Christ.

---

[1] "Ordination of Priests," in *Rites of Ordination of a Bishop, of Priests, and of Deacons*, 2nd ed. (Washington, DC: United States Conference of Catholic Bishops, 2003), no. 122.

[2] "Ordination of a Bishop," *Rites of Ordination*, no. 40.

Why Do We Call This the Sacrament of Orders?

According to the *Catechism of the Catholic Church*, holy orders is the sacrament through which the mission entrusted by Christ to his apostles continues to be exercised in the church until the end of time.[3] Each of the seven sacraments provides a unique means to encounter Christ through a prescribed ritual action. The sacrament of orders achieves this through the "ordering" of the membership of the church.

For a community to thrive it needs order. From a tribal clan to a nation-state, wise leaders are needed for faithful followers. Good order finds a middle ground between extremes of anarchy and fascism. In a state of nature, people tend to pursue their self-interest, taking advantage of others while satisfying their own needs and desires. Under fascism, a strict domineering order is imposed, a crushing uniformity which stifles the creativity of society's diverse members. A good order creates harmony throughout a community, enabling its members to flourish, developing their abilities to the fullest, all for the greater good of the whole. Talented ones are encouraged to excel while the lesser able are supported. From this state of interdependence some will rise to positions of leadership—hopefully those who display an understanding of the story of the community, its history, and its destiny. The good leader is also able to recognize differing abilities within the group and harness them for the greater good of all. Communities thrive on such order. The church is one such community.

It was the intention of Jesus of Nazareth to found such an ordered community, as he declares to his disciple, "You are Peter, and on this rock I will build my church" (Matt 16:18). The evangelist Matthew uses the Greek word *ecclesia* for "church," which literally means "gathering." Throughout his earthly ministry, Jesus charged his disciples to continue his work, missioning them to heal the sick and forgive sins in his name. Before leaving his disciples, he promised to send them the *paraclete*, the Holy Spirit, to guide them, and he commanded the disciples to travel the world, teaching what he taught them and baptizing as he baptized. His disciples became the apostles

---

[3] *Catechism of the Catholic Church*. ed. United States Catholic Conference. (Allen, TX: Thomas More, 1994), 1536.

who continued the mission of Jesus Christ in word and deed, and the church grew. St. Luke records that on the feast of Pentecost, after the spectacular descent of the Spirit, three thousand people joined the church (see Acts 2:41). Through the tireless efforts of missionary apostles like St. Paul, this church expanded throughout Asia Minor and North Africa and to Rome. To foster the growth of community, order was needed. To meet this need, three positions arose, *episkopoi* (overseers), *presbyters* (elders), and *diakonoi* (ministers or servants). Up to the middle of the second century CE, the first two titles were employed interchangeably. Unlike the missionary work of the first apostles, these elders remained closer to home and to their twofold responsibility of maintaining economy and orthodoxy. They managed the affairs of the community and they promoted the proper teaching of Christ and the apostles while preventing heretical ideas from polluting this teaching. The deacons—literally "table servers"—tended to the concerns of community members, ensuring that all had enough to eat. These three positions became known as "orders," for they were responsible for providing order within the church community.

But they were not the only orders. In the early church, many orders existed. St. Paul lists several of them when he writes, "God has appointed in the church first apostles, second prophets, third teachers; then deeds of power, then gifts of healing, forms of assistance, forms of leadership, various kinds of tongues" (1 Cor 12:28). Paul refers to these works as "gifts." Moreover, they were considered to be charisms because the bearer of these gifts exuded a "charisma," that is, a power given to a person by God, granting one authority and an ability to exercise leadership. All of these charisms were necessary for building up the body of Christ.

The system of ordering is derived from ancient Roman society and refers to an established civil body, especially a governing body. "Ordination" refers to a ceremony of incorporation into an "order," which was accompanied by a ritual of blessing. Within the civil body, or "order," were several groups that functioned together for the greater good of the whole. The Christian Church was strongly influenced by the Roman system of government, and so the faithful were "ordered" for the greater glory of God. This order is expressed in the Liturgy of the Eucharist. When we pray Eucharistic Prayer III, the priest says: "Be pleased to confirm in faith and charity your pilgrim Church on earth, with your servant N. our Pope, and N. our Bishop, the Order of Bishops, all the clergy, and the entire people you have gained for your own." This list is no mere roll call of the hierarchy. Rather, it expresses the church's unity through the ordering of the members.[4]

In our discussion we will focus on the order of priesthood. The Roman Catholic priesthood finds its roots in the Old Testament. From the beginning, all Israel was looked on as "a kingdom of priests, a holy nation." Eventually, the tribe of Levi was designated for liturgical service, priests consecrated to act on behalf of the nation (See Heb 5:1; Exod 29:1-30; Lev 8). They served a threefold function: first, to discern God's will and interpret it for the Israelites; second, to teach in order to maintain the tradition; and third, to offer sacrifice for the sins of the Israelites to effect atonement on their behalf. The priestly tribe of Levi served as intermediaries between God and the people of Israel.

Within the early Christian community, however, we do not find such "priests." The New Testament does not talk of priests except in the Letter to the Hebrews, in which Jesus is called the "High Priest." The apostles, in describing their work among various communities, never refer to themselves as presiding at the celebration of the Eucharist. Someone must have presided, but whoever it was is not mentioned. Nevertheless, it was under the supervision of the presbyters that the many ministries of the Christian community flourished.

Beginning in the second century CE, we discern a shift, that is, a decline of the diverse ministries throughout the community and the emergence of the threefold ministry of bishop, priest, and deacon. This was due in part to the expansion of Christianity, to the establishment of numerous churches, and to the need for presbyters to lead them. Also at this time, we find a shift in the understanding of the Eucharist to greater emphasis on its sacrificial nature. Consequently, many diverse ministries were consolidated into the order of the presbyterate. The community was thus separated into two distinct groups. Now, a large group of laity were directed by a small group of the ordained. The priesthood consolidated the diverse roles of the early church. The distinction between the two groups gradually developed into a pyramid, with influence flowing from the top downward.[4]

---

[4] Thomas O'Meara, "Orders and Ordination," in *The New Dictionary of Theology*, ed. Joseph Komanchak, Mary Collins, and Dermot Lane (Wilmington, DE: Michael Glazier Press, 1987), 724.

The Development of the Cultic Priesthood

Another shift in the ordering of the church occurred as clergy acquired both sacred and secular authority, beginning with the Edict of Constantine (313 CE). With this proclamation, bishops and priests came to enjoy the privileges of civic officials. The Rite of Ordination reflected this secular authority. Modeled on the coronation of a prince, the bishop was given a staff (crozier) and a ring and sat on a throne. A priest was ordained with an anointing of his hands and then handed the bread and wine. It was during this era that the presbyterate began to be viewed more as priesthood with the power to consecrate and offer the sacrifice of Christ's body and blood. This became the definition of the sacrament of orders.[5]

Sometime later, in the sixteenth century CE, the notion of a cultic priesthood was reinforced by the Protestant Reformation (1517). Reformers argued that ordination empowered a minister only to preach the Gospel and care for the faithful, not to offer the sacrifice of the Eucharist. In response, the Council of Trent (1563) taught that priests reflect the image of Christ the High Priest and that they are consecrated for a threefold purpose: to preach the Gospel, to shepherd the faithful, and to celebrate divine worship.[6] Eventually, the Catholic hierarchy came to emphasize the priest's role in the Eucharist, with the other two purposes becoming less important.

Just as the order of the church was influenced by the structure of its day, it was influenced by the philosophical vision common to the Middle Ages, within which, all of creation participates in divine truth to varying degrees. Those with a higher degree of participation influence those of lower degree. In this way, all of creation is ordered. This universal law of creation was reflected in the order of ministries within the church. The faithful received the grace of God through the ministry of the ordained. The ordained were ranked in descending

---

[5] David Power, "Order," in *Systematic Theology: Roman Catholic Perspectives*, ed. Francis Schüssler Fiorenza and John Galvin, vol. 2 (Minneapolis, MN: Fortress Press, 1991), 299. See also, Richard P. McBrien, *Catholicism* (San Francisco: Harper and Row, 1981), 804–5.

[6] "The General Council of Trent, Twenty-Third Session, Doctrine on the Sacrament of Order," in *The Christian Faith in the Doctrinal Documents of the Catholic Church*, ed. J. Neuner and J. Dupuis (New York: Alba House, 1982); see also, Michael Lawler, *A Theology of Ministry* (Kansas City, MO: Sheed and Ward, 1990), 82.

order: bishop, presbyter, and deacon, according to their participation in sacred power. Both the political and philosophical worldviews gave rise to clericalism within the church. Clericalism treats ordained ministers as an "elite corps" bearing sole responsibility for the church's mission, absorbing ecclesial power and privilege while the laity remain passive participants in this mission.[7] This pyramid order held fast until the twentieth century.

Restoring the Order: The Second Vatican Council

The Second Vatican Council (1962–1965) urged a restoration of the relationship between the ordained and the laity. Much of the work of the council was a process of *ressourcement*, i.e., a return to the sources; the church engaged in an investigation of the doctrines and worship of early Christian communities for the purpose of renewing the contemporary church. To be sure, this was not a matter of claiming that whatever was done in the past was best. But, for the institution to preserve its tradition, it needed to take one step backward before taking two steps forward.

In stepping backward, we are reminded of the relationship between the ordained and the laity, most notably through a renewed emphasis on a common baptism. The sacrament of baptism is the foundation for the sacrament of orders, for it is through the initiation with water and chrism that the priesthood of all believers is established, as we read in 1 Peter, "a chosen race, a royal priesthood, a holy nation, God's own people" (1 Pet 2:9). The ordained minister is first and foremost a member of the baptized community. In the words of Augustine, "For you I am a bishop, but with you I am a Christian."[8]

All Christians share in the mission of the one High Priest, Jesus Christ, for in baptism, these words were spoken over them: "As Christ was anointed Priest, Prophet, and King, so may you live always as a member of his body, sharing everlasting life."[9] Moreover, we read in the council's document *Lumen Gentium*, "the baptized, by regeneration

---

[7] Power, "Order," 298. See also, Susan Wood, *Sacramental Orders*, Lex Orandi Series (Collegeville, MN: Liturgical Press, 2000), 4.

[8] *Sermo* 340. See Lawler, *Theology of Ministry*, 87.

[9] "Rite of Christian Initiation for Adults," *Rites*, no. 224.

and anointing of the Holy Spirit, are consecrated into a spiritual house and a holy priesthood" (LG 10). To be sure, the council fathers explain there is an essential difference between the ordained priesthood and the priesthood of the baptized: the ordained enjoy a "sacred power" to act in the person of Christ, offering the eucharistic sacrifice to God in the name of all the people. Nevertheless, the two are interrelated. Thirty-four years later, Pope John Paul II noted the need for a careful rereading of the council's teaching concerning the relationship between the priesthood of the faithful and the ministerial priesthood. In his words, "This relationship corresponds to the structure of the church as a community. The priesthood is not an institution that exists alongside the laity or above it. The priesthood of the bishop, priest, (and) deacon, is for the laity and precisely for this reason it possesses a ministerial character, that is, one of service." [10] The characterization of service contrasts with the identity of the cultic priesthood and its focus on offering the sacrifice of the Eucharist.

With the reform of the church in the twentieth century came a renewal of the duties of preaching the Word of God, leading the community, and presiding at the Eucharist. Indeed, in *Presbyterorum Ordinis* (the Decree on the Ministry and Life of Priests) the council states that the primary duty for priests is the proclamation of the Gospel of God to all (see PO 4). Priests are to live among the people of the world as good shepherds and as such should know their sheep. Moreover, while they owe service to everyone, they should show special care to the community's poorest and the weakest members. This notion was further developed by American bishops as the preferential option for the poor. The act of showing special care for the *anawim*, a Hebrew word meaning "poor and lowly," makes visible the gospel passage of the final judgment, in which Jesus states, "Truly I tell you, just as you did it to one of the least of these who are members of my family, you did it to me" (Matt 25:40). So, while priests are set apart from the community with the special role of preaching, leading, and worshiping, they are to see themselves more as members of the same body of Christ, assuming more the role of a servant. In the words of the council, "They should unite their efforts with those of the lay faithful and conduct themselves among them after the

[10] John Paul II, "Holy Thursday letter to Priests," April 12, 1990.

example of the master who came among them 'not to be served but to serve, and to give his life as a ransom for many' " (PO 3, 5, 9). Interestingly, of the three ranks of the ordained—bishop, priest, and deacon—Jesus seems to identify more with the deacon and the position of service. This is also illustrated at the Last Supper, when he assumed the position of the servant and washed the feet of his disciples. He reminded them repeatedly that the greatest among them will be ready to serve the least (see John 13:1-16; Luke 22:26).

Maintaining a Just Relationship: Justice and Orders

Justice is concerned with maintaining right relationships. For the purpose of our discussion, we are concerned with the relationship between the ordained ministers and the priesthood of the baptized. In order to understand justice and its relation to the sacrament of orders, we will distinguish biblical justice from social justice. Social justice, i.e., the way justice is practiced in American society, is a matter of contractual agreement, based on *quid pro quo*. It may be in the form of a business contract in which two parties sign a written agreement promising to fulfill certain conditions, or a social contract in which the citizens abide by a code of behavior and in return enjoy the privileges and protection of the government. In this way, social justice is contractual. But in the world of the Bible, justice is considered to be a gift from God. Regina Schwartz expresses well the distinction between these two in asking, "Does justice come from some rational understanding that our will cannot be done without compromise with the wills of others, some recognition of the necessity of essentially contractual relationships . . . or is its source some higher desire to make the world a good place to secure the world through acts of justice?" [11] God breaks into the world, intruding into human history, and establishes a covenant with humanity. In this covenant, God promises to care for his people like a loving parent, asking his people only to remain faithful to him in return. Thus, biblical justice is relational, requiring the faithful to take responsibility for their place within the covenant and to demonstrate through actions their fidelity

---

[11] Regina Schwartz, *Sacramental Poetics at the Dawn of Secularism: When God Left the World* (Stanford, CA: Stanford University Press, 2008), 39.

to God.[12] In short, justice requires us to take responsibility for our relationships, because in remaining faithful we are drawn closer to God. As the prophet Jeremiah says, "He [your father] judged the cause of the poor and needy; then it was well. Is not this to know me? says the Lord" (Jer 22:16). Fidelity is the life of righteousness, i.e., living in right relationship with God.

How does the ordained priest practice justice? By working for the proper order in the church. His job description is laid out in the bishop's homily for the Rite of Ordination:

> It is true that God has made his entire holy people a royal priesthood in Christ. Nevertheless, our great Priest himself, Jesus Christ, chose certain disciples to carry out publicly in his name, and on behalf of mankind, a priestly office in the Church. For Christ was sent by the Father and he in turn sent the Apostles into the world, so that through them and their successors, the Bishops, he might continue to exercise his office of Teacher, Priest, and Shepherd. Indeed, priests are established co-workers of the Order of Bishops, with whom they are joined in the priestly office and with whom they are called to the service of the people of God. . . . In being configured to Christ the eternal High Priest and joined to the priesthood of the Bishops, they will be consecrated as true priests of the New Testament, to preach the Gospel, to shepherd God's people, and to celebrate the sacred Liturgy, especially the Lord's sacrifice.[13]

The bishop's homily makes clear that ordained ministers rise from the ranks of the priesthood of the baptized whole. Church teaching makes clear that the "royal priesthood" of all the faithful participates in the priesthood of Christ, each one in his or her own proper way. Within this royal priesthood, "The ministerial priesthood is at the service of the common priesthood, directed at the unfolding of the baptismal grace of all Christians."[14]

As we stated at the beginning, every community needs to be ordered for the sake of maintaining unity and harmony and to enable the community to grow. Recall how Paul compares the mystical body

---

[12] For a fine discussion of biblical justice, see John Donahue, *What Does the Lord Require? A Bibliographical Essay on the Bible and Social Justice*, Series 4, Studies in Jesuit Topics (St. Louis, MO: Institute of Jesuit Sources, 2000).

[13] "Ordination of Priests," *Rites of Ordination*, no. 123.

[14] *Catechism of the Catholic Church*, 1547.

of Christ—the Christian community—to the human body (see 1 Cor 12:12-31). In doing so he points out the fallacy of one body part arguing for its superiority over any part. If the toe aches, the whole body feels pain. Each part of the human body has its function in maintaining the harmony for the whole—so too in the church that strives for unity and harmony among the diversity of ministries. For this reason, we can say the church does not *have* a hierarchy so much as the church *is* a hierarchy. In this hierarchy, the members do not share the same roles, but each plays a part that cannot be fully appreciated apart from the others.[15] We may recall Jesus' prayer for his disciples before his arrest, "Holy Father, protect them in your name that you have given me, so that they may be one, as we are one" (John 17:11). In the communion of Christians, Christ is made manifest in a unique way.

For the church, this order is made visible in the Liturgy of the Eucharist. The liturgy symbolizes communion, our relationship with one another and with God. It is here that we express the mystery of Christ and the purpose of the church: "The celebration of the Mass, as the action of Christ and of the People of God arrayed hierarchically, is the center of the whole of Christian life."[16] For this reason, the celebration of the Mass should be so ordered with the ministers and faithful participating according to their proper roles. The purpose for this ordering is to foster the full, conscious, and active participation of all the faithful.[17]

Order in the Future Church

Given that the liturgy is the central act of the Christian life, may we consider the subject of restricting ordination to celibate men? For the Roman Catholic Church, all ordained ministers, except for permanent deacons, are required to be men of faith who live a celibate life.[18] The purpose in this discussion is neither to challenge the role of celibacy, nor argue for the ordination of women. However, we need

[15] See Brian Dunn, "*Sacramentum Concilium* and the Call to Holiness," *Worship* 86, no. 4 (July 2012): 343–44.

[16] "General Instruction of the Roman Missal," in *The Roman Missal, Third Edition* (Collegeville, MN: Liturgical Press, 2011), no. 16.

[17] Ibid., nos. 16–18.

[18] *Catechism of the Catholic Church*, 1577, 1579.

to ask, for the sake of justice, how important is celibacy to the celebration of the Eucharist?

Pope Benedict XVI described eloquently the importance of "the Sunday obligation" in his encyclical *Sacramentum Caritatis*.[19] "Participating in the Sunday liturgical assembly with all our brothers and sisters, with whom we form one body in Jesus Christ, is demanded by our Christian conscience and at the same time it forms that conscience. To lose a sense of Sunday as the Lord's Day, a day to be sanctified, is symptomatic of the loss of an authentic sense of Christian freedom" (*Sacramentum Caritatis* 73). Even so, the pope recognized the worldwide problem of a lack of priests and that for many Christians, it is impossible to celebrate the Eucharist on the Lord's Day. In these cases, he recommended that those able to travel to another church in the diocese where there is a priest do so, even if the journey demanded a sacrifice. For those people for whom it is impossible to find a priest, they are asked to commemorate this day with a celebration of the Liturgy of the Word followed by the distribution of communion. In such services, it is advised that competent lay ministers be chosen who should be careful not to "obscure the indispensable ministry of priests." We are asked also to pray that the Lord will send more priests to tend the harvest of the faithful. Would that we could see more priests responding to this call. But for now, the number of future priests shrinks as the age of current priests advances. Meanwhile, poorer Catholics throughout the world worship without a priest, missing the opportunity for the celebration of the Eucharist.

Yet we remain a eucharistic church. It is the Eucharist, with the faithful hierarchically arrayed, that defines us. In light of this, two values emerge which conflict with one another. On one hand, the church maintains the tradition of restricting ordination to celibate men. On the other, the church finds it necessary to remind the faithful of the importance of the Sunday celebration of the Eucharist. In weighing these two values, the scale currently tips toward the first. Do we really mean to say that male celibacy outweighs Sunday

---

[19] "*Sacramentum Caritatis*: The Sacrament of Love" (Strathfield, NSW: St. Paul's Publications, 2007). In his description of the significance of Sunday for Christians, Pope Benedict continues the message of John Paul II from *Dies Domini*.

Eucharist? Stretching the issue, Dominican theologian Edward Schillebeeckx opined that there really is no shortage of priests but a shortage of men who wish to be ordained and live a celibate life.[20] If we consider the custom of the early church, in which presbyters were responsible for recognizing the charisms held by the members of the community, encouraging people to develop them for the good of the community and for the glory of God, could we recognize in the church today the ability to preach the Gospel, lead the faithful, and celebrate the liturgy, in many more members? Is it right and just that so many go without being nourished by the Eucharist?

---

[20] Edward Schillebeeckx, *The Church with a Human Face: A New and Expanded Theology of Ministry* (New York: Crossroad, 1985), 240.

7

Anointing of the Sick and Justice

Paul Turner

Tears spilled from Gabi's old eyes as she gasped for breath and stuttered her deepest fear: "I just hope God is not angry with me."

Looking around her small urban home, walls covered with religious art and family photos, shelves crowded with devotional articles, books, and spiritually themed CDs, with a televangelist vying with me for Gabi's attention, I couldn't imagine how on earth—or in heaven for that matter—God could be angry with this elderly woman, faithful to the church her entire life in spite of family strife and economic disparity, longing for the strength to leave her confinement and go to the one place that meant the most to her.

Not the grocery store. Not the beauty parlor. Not even her children's homes. Gabi wanted to go to church. She wanted to participate in Mass again. She wanted to pray first Saturday devotions with her friends, but she couldn't. An injury to her leg made it difficult for her to stand, and she feared she could not walk without falling again.

Multiple trips to the doctor provided little relief from the multitude of ailments afflicting her. Unable to drive, reliant on the goodwill of others, Gabi accepted weekly Communion at home from another parishioner whose own spiritual life had been strengthened by Gabi's. "She's the most spiritual person I've ever met," Evelyn told me.

Sitting in Gabi's living room, prepared to offer the anointing of the sick, I struggled to reconcile how the most spiritual person one Catholic has ever met could carry horrific fears that God is angry with her. It all has to do with the complex of physical, emotional, and spiritual concerns that rise unjustly when a person gets sick.

History

Today's sacrament of the anointing of the sick rose from a long history of the Catholic Church's administration of pastoral care. Two key Scripture passages inspired the practice: the disciples anointing the sick as part of their ministry (Mark 6:13) and James commanding the sick to call for the presbyters of the church to be anointed (Jas 5:14-16).

Beyond this explicit testimony, Jesus demonstrated extraordinary care for the sick throughout his ministry; at the end of his life he foresaw that those on whom the apostles laid hands would recover (Mark 16:18). In his prophetic ministry, Jesus' care of the sick telescoped his larger ministry and message: he came to save the whole human person. The return of one's physical health foreshadowed one's resurrection. Jesus' ministry also demonstrated his care for those on the fringes of society—including lepers, the paralyzed, the blind, and those possessed by demons.

Jesus and the apostles enjoyed some success in treating the sick, but not every sick person was restored to health. Reconciling the success and failure of healer and healed widened the early church's early theological perspective on the purpose of illness. Those destined to share rewards with Christ should expect to share his sufferings. Paul wrote that Christians were joint heirs with Christ if they suffered with him (Rom 8:17). He argued further, "I am now rejoicing in my sufferings for your sake, and in my flesh I am completing what is lacking in Christ's afflictions for the sake of his body, that is, the church" (Col 1:24). For Paul, Christian suffering continued and completed the saving suffering of Jesus Christ. This sentiment recurs in 1 Peter, which urged Christians to rejoice to the extent that they share in the sufferings of Christ because they will share in his glory (1 Pet

4:13). This thinking helped Christians find meaning in suffering that seemed otherwise unfair. Suffering is not good on its own, but it stakes the path to glory.

Justin Martyr (d. 165 CE) reports a practice that may represent early pastoral care of the sick. At the Eucharist, after the faithful shared Communion, deacons distributed some of what remained so that people could bring Communion to those absent.[1] Very likely, he means to the sick. Around the same time, Polycarp of Smyrna admonished presbyters to visit the sick.[2] The fourth-century *Canons of Hippolytus* encouraged bishops to do the same.[3] From the earliest centuries, the church brought hope to those tempted to despair.

After the biblical testimony, the earliest clear reference to anointing the sick comes from the *Apostolic Tradition*, a church order probably dating to the fourth century CE. In the course of a ceremony detailed there, the bishop prays that God will sanctify oil and give health to those using and receiving it.[4] Additional evidence comes from the same century: Rufinus tells of desert fathers and monks who anointed for healing, though he says nothing of them using oil previously blessed by a bishop.[5] Aphraates knew of oil that "perfects those who are anointed (priests, kings, and prophets), anoints the sick, and in a hidden and mysterious way brings back those who repent."[6] The *Apostolic Constitutions* include a prayer asking God to make water and oil effective in "producing health, driving out sicknesses, putting

---

[1] See the *Catechism of the Catholic Church*, ed. United States Catholic Conference (Allen, TX: Thomas More, 1994), 1345.

[2] A. G. Martimort, "Prayer for the Sick and Sacramental Anointing," in *The Church at Prayer: An Introduction to the Liturgy*, ed. Aimé Martimort, vol. 3, The Sacraments (Collegeville, MN: Liturgical Press, 1992), 123.

[3] Ibid.

[4] Paul F. Bradshaw, Maxwell E. Johnson and L. Edward Phillips, *The Apostolic Tradition: A Commentary*, Hermeneia 85 (Minneapolis, MN: Fortress Press, 2002), 5:2, 50.

[5] Rufinus of Aquileia, *In suam et Eusebii Caesariensis Latinam ab eo factam historiam*; PL 21:112–13.

[6] *Exposition on the Grape*, Sources chrétiennes 359 (Paris, 1989), 2:880–81. Cited in Stefano Parenti, "Anointing of the Sick During the First Four Centuries," in *Handbook for Liturgical Studies Volume 4: Sacraments and Sacramentals*, ed. Anscar J. Chupungco (Collegeville, MN: Liturgical Press, 2000), 156–57.

demons to flight, and foiling ambushes."[7] A similar prayer appears in the *Euchologion of Serapion*, a prayer book from Egypt.[8]

In the fifth century CE, the *Testamentum Domini* includes a prayer blessing oil for various purposes: "that it may deliver those who labor and heal those who are sick, and sanctify those who return, when they draw near to your faith."[9] Legislation governing anointing stems first from the letter of Pope Innocent I to Decentius of Gubbio in 416. Innocent resorted to the Letter of James to justify various practices. He explicitly states that the bishop prepared the oil, that not only priests but also all Christians could anoint, and that they could anoint themselves or others.[10]

This testimony demonstrates that prayerful anointing was not restricted to those with a physical illness. It also was intended for those enduring societal and spiritual conflicts, and the bishop prayed over at least some of the oil used to set both groups of sufferers free from whatever kept them bound.

In Eastern rites, a variety of rituals emerged, sharing some of those features of anointing practiced in the West. By the Middle Ages, the Byzantine Rite celebrated anointing either during or outside of Mass. Seven priests could celebrate the Rite together, or one could repeat it over seven days. Anointing with a brush had become common, and priests laid a Book of the Gospels on the head of the sick.[11] Evidence for Eastern practice in this period remains scant, but it indicates few distinctions between the oil of catechumens and the oil of the sick, between anointing and penance, or even between anointing the living and anointing the dead.[12] This may suggest imprecision but more likely shows the diverse ways the church prayed for the restoration of those experiencing loss.

In the Latin Rite, the bishop's text for blessing oil evolved from the seventh-century Gelasian Sacramentary: "Send, we pray, O Lord, the Holy Spirit, the Paraclete, from heaven on this lotion of oil, which

---

[7] Martimort, "Prayer for the Sick," 120.

[8] Ibid.

[9] *The Apostolic Tradition*, 53.

[10] DS 216.

[11] Martimort, "Prayer for the Sick," 125.

[12] Ibid., 126. See also the treatment in Parenti, "Care and Anointing of the Sick in the East," in *Handbook for Liturgical Studies*, 161–69.

you have been pleased to bring forth from the green tree for the restoring of mind and body. And may your holy blessing be a protection of body, mind, and spirit for all anointing, tasting, and touching, for eliminating all sorrows, all sickness, all illness of mind and body."[13] A simpler and probably more original version appears in the Gregorian Sacramentary of the eighth century.[14] Inspired by the practice in the *Apostolic Tradition*, this prayer appears near the end of the Canon of the Mass as part of the blessings of various items people brought to the church to indicate the sacrifice of themselves to God. The prayer built on the church's enduring concern for the healing of the whole person.

Growing legislation formalized the anointing ritual during the time of Charlemagne. The Roman practice of the bishop to bless the oil at the chrism Mass gradually spread throughout the West. As in the East, several priests could perform the same ceremony, probably because the Letter of James encouraged the sick to summon the "presbyters" of the church. Laypeople were no longer allowed to administer the oil of the sick; the last reference to the practice came about 720 CE from Bede the Venerable, who still relied on the legislation of Innocent I.[15] The order of service progressed from sprinkling holy water to confession, communion, and blessing the sick person.[16] The prayers for anointing also began to include hand laying. The earliest known formula for anointing came from Ireland, "I anoint you with sanctified oil in the name of the Trinity that you may be saved for ever and ever."[17] Rubrics began to specify which body parts should be anointed.[18] What the period lost by narrowing the variations, it balanced with perceived best practices on behalf of those in need.

---

[13] Leo Cunibert Mohlberg, ed., *Liber Sacramentorum Romanae Aeclesiae ordinis anni circuli* (Rome: Casa Editrice Herder, 1981), 382; my translation.

[14] Jean Despises, ed., *Le Sacramentaire Grégorien* (Fribourg: Editions universities Fribourg, 1979), 334.

[15] Parenti, "Care and Anointing," 173, citing Bede the Venerable, *The Commentary on the Seven Catholic Epistles*, ed. and trans. D. Hurst, Cistercian Studies 82 (Kalamazoo, MI: Cistercian Publications, 1985), 61–62.

[16] Martimort, "Prayer for the Sick," 128.

[17] Ibid., 129; my translation.

[18] Ibid., 130.

In time, the anointing became associated with prayers for the dying. Restricting its administration to priests spotlighted its penitential aspects, which fostered a transformation from deliverance from physical illness to deliverance from sin. In associating anointing with penitence, people were waiting for the end of their lives to confess their sins and receive anointing. The expression "extreme unction" may have originally referred to the final anointing in the series begun with prebaptismal rites, but it became more generally understood as the last anointing one received before dying.[19] The term appeared in theological commentary and canonical collections as early as the twelfth century, but it did not enter the ritual until the fifteenth century.[20] The Second Council of Lyons, which first defined the seven sacraments of the Catholic Church in 1274, included "extreme unction" among them.[21] Thus, by the time it first entered the list of sacraments, its purpose was understood less for deliverances from physical, social, and spiritual duress than for one's final deliverance from death to salvation.

In the sixteenth century the Council of Trent combined the sacraments of penance and extreme unction, considering the latter a complement to the former.[22] The council, citing the Letter of James, stressed that the proper ministers are "presbyters" of the church, which it interpreted to mean bishops or priests.[23] Still referring to James, the council declared that "this anointing pertains to the sick, but especially to those who are so perilously impaired that they seem to have reached the end of life."[24] Thus, Trent did not limit anointing to those who were dying, but in practice its association with death remained.

The Roman Ritual of 1614 had separate chapters for viaticum (communion for the dying) and the sacrament of extreme unction. Viaticum was given before anointing. To administer extreme unction, the priest on entering the room said, "Peace to this house." He sprinkled holy water. He offered a series of prayers, and the penitent ordinarily made

[19] Parenti, "Care and Anointing," 175–76.
[20] Martimort, "Prayer for the Sick," 131.
[21] DS 860.
[22] DS 1694.
[23] DS 1697.
[24] DS 1698; my translation.

a general confession. The seven penitential psalms were recited, then the litany of the saints, and prayers during the anointing. Extending his right hand over the head of the sick person, the priest asked God to extinguish the power of the devil. He then anointed the eyes, ears, nose, closed lips, hands, and feet, saying each time, "Through this holy anointing, and his most loving mercy, may the Lord be indulgent to you for whatever you lack through 'sight,' 'hearing,' 'smell,' 'taste and speech,' 'touch,' and 'step.' "[25] The verbs "be indulgent" and "lack" refer to God having mercy on one's physical weakness and, at least, imply God's forgiveness of spiritual sin. Sick priests were to be anointed on the outside of their hands rather than the palms, probably to avoid any confusion with the anointing received at ordination. A series of prayers in dialogue then preceded a sequence of orations. The priest could then encourage the sick person to prepare for death before he sprinkled the person with holy water and presented a cross for veneration. Finally, he asked the caretakers to summon a priest at the moment of death. In practice, the Rite was completely concerned with the pastoral care of the dying.

Unsurprisingly, when canon law was codified in 1917, it restricted the administration of this sacrament to those "who by an appropriate use of reason have turned because of infirmity or old age to danger of death."[26] Pope Benedict XV broadened the interpretation in a 1921 apostolic letter addressed to the sodality of *Bona Mors*. He urged people not to delay viaticum and extreme unction until the sick were about to lose consciousness. "On the contrary, according to the teaching and the precepts of the Church, they should be strengthened by these sacraments as soon as their condition worsens and one may prudently judge that there is danger of death."[27] Two years later, Pope Pius XI said, "A prudent or reasonably sure judgment, without scruple, is sufficient for deciding on the seriousness of an illness."[28]

Thus the groundwork was laid for an expansion of pastoral care to the suffering after the Second Vatican Council (1962–1965). The council's *Sacrosanctum Concilium* (the Constitution on the Sacred

---

[25] *Rituale Romanum* (Rome: Desclée & Cie, 1952), 202; my translation.

[26] *Corpus iuris canonici* (Westminster: The Newman Press, 1952), 940; my translation.

[27] J. Neuner and J. Dupuis, eds., *The Christian Faith in the Doctrinal Documents of the Catholic Church*, rev. ed. (London: Collins, 1983), 1661.

[28] "Pastoral Care of the Sick: Rites of Anointing and Viaticum," 8, in *The Rites of the Catholic Church*, vol. 1 (Collegeville, MN: Liturgical Press, 1990), 780.

Liturgy) asked to change the name of the sacrament from "extreme unction" to "anointing of the sick": it would no longer pertain only to those on the point of death. "As soon as any of the faithful begins to be in danger of death from sickness or old age, this is already a suitable time" for the sacrament (SC 73). The council asked for a revision of the separate rites for anointing and viaticum and for the preparation of a continuous rite for these sacraments, though in this new sequence: confession, anointing, and viaticum (SC 74). The council decided that the number of anointings should suit the occasion—not everyone needed multiple anointings of body parts. Finally, the prayers were to be revised "to correspond to the varying conditions of the sick people who receive the sacrament" (SC 75). All of these changes brought the sacrament closer to the diverse needs of the sick and clarified its purpose in relation to other ceremonies of the church.

In *Lumen Gentium* (the Dogmatic Constitution on the Church), the council restated these overarching goals in two significant phrases:

> By the sacred Anointing of the Sick and the prayer of the priests, the whole church commends those who are ill to the suffering and glorified Lord that he may give them relief and save them (see Jas 5:14-16). And indeed, it exhorts them to contribute to the good of the people of God by freely uniting themselves to the passion and death of Christ (see Rom 8:17; Col 1:24; 2 Tim 2:11-12; 1 Pet 4:13). (LG 11)

On the one hand, the sick would benefit from relief and salvation; on the other hand, they would contribute to the church by uniting themselves to the passion and death of Christ. These realistic appraisals demonstrate the church's wider pastoral care for the sick.

As anointing is part of the church's ministry to the sick, so ministry to the sick is part of the church's mission to perform charitable works. The council listed such works as one objective for the apostolate of laypeople. Christ made charity part of his disciples' work. In *Apostolicam Actuositatem* (the Decree on the Apostolate of Lay People) the council wrote,

> While rejoicing at initiatives taken elsewhere, [the church] claims charitable works as its own mission and right. That is why mercy to the poor and the sick, charitable works and works of mutual aid for the alleviation of all kinds of human need, are especially esteemed in the church. (AA 8)

In light of these directives, the task of revising the Rite fell to Study Group 23 of the Consilium for Implementing the Constitution on the Sacred Liturgy. Headed by Pierre-Marie Gy, the director of the Liturgical Institute of Paris, with the Italian parish priest Secondo Mazzarello as secretary, the members were Jairo Mejia, a priest from Colombia; Canon Jean Rabau, a parish priest from Belgium; Johannes Hofinger, an Austrian Jesuit and director of the East Asian Pastoral Institute in Manila; François Vandenbroucke, a Belgian Benedictine; and Damien Sicard, a priest from France. Later members were Antoine Chavasse, a priest at the University of Strasbourg, France; Bruno Löwenberg, a priest from Germany; and Korbinian Ritzer, a German Benedictine.[29] This group consulted professors on the faculty of medicine at Paris and Louvain, and in Italy and Germany, as well as specialists in the pastoral care of the sick, especially at Lourdes.[30]

Study Group 23 immediately examined the sacramental formula. "The existing formula brought out the negative effect of the sacrament, namely, deliverance from sin, but was less clear on the positive effect, namely, the spiritual and even the physical relief of the sick person."[31] The pope personally has to approve a proposal to change any sacramental formula, and Paul VI responded favorably to this request.

When the council clarified the purpose of the sacrament, it broadened the conditions for the faithful to receive it. Some illnesses are serious but not immediately dangerous. The advance of medical treatments now allow a person with a dangerous illness to survive much longer than before.[32] The Congregation for the Doctrine of the Faith steered a middle course, saying, "the anointing of the sick is neither a sacrament for the dying nor a religious remedy for any and every illness."[33] People could then be anointed more than once for the same illness in its various stages.

The resulting rite "is more than an updating of the old. It also brings together in organic fashion all the activities that the Church performs in its effort to stand by the sick, support and help them

---

[29] Annibale Bugnini, *The Reform of the Liturgy 1948–1975*, trans. Matthew J. O'Connell (Collegeville, MN: Liturgical Press, 1990), 579, 684.

[30] Ibid., 684.

[31] Ibid., 685.

[32] Ibid., 686.

[33] Ibid., 687.

spiritually, and accompany them as they complete their own paschal mystery in conformity to Christ."[34]

The revised rite is aptly called Pastoral Care of the Sick: Rites of Anointing and Viaticum.[35] Situated within the embrace of the church's care for the sick, the specific rites of anointing the sick and Communion for the dying attract other attendant liturgies, from visiting the sick to baptizing a person in danger of death.

The introductory material includes a decree from the Sacred Congregation for Divine Worship, which states that this ministry continues that of Jesus.[36] The Apostolic Constitution of Pope Paul VI traces a history of the sacrament and cites directives from the Second Vatican Council. The pope authorized the use of any vegetable oil, no longer requiring olive oil, so difficult to obtain in some parts of the world. He also authorized the revised formula: "Through this holy anointing / May the Lord in His love and mercy help you with the grace of the Holy Spirit. / May the Lord who frees you from sin / save you and raise you up."[37] The reference to the Holy Spirit here and in other prayers shows the influence of the Eastern rites on the liturgical renewal in the West.[38]

The General Introduction addresses the difficult question of human suffering. It balances a belief that sickness has meaning with the hope that Christ can heal. It speaks of the positive role of the sick within the church. It permits an anointing before surgery for a serious illness. In keeping with canon law, it permits the anointing of children who have the use of reason, though it tolerates anointing younger children. The introduction also notes the role of the entire community in offering care to the sick.[39]

The main part of the revised rite divides into two parts—pastoral care of the sick, and pastoral care of the dying. The first part includes visits to the sick; visits to a sick child; communion of the sick, whether in ordinary circumstances or in a hospital or institution; and anointing of the sick outside or within Mass, or in a hospital or institution. The second part includes the celebration of viaticum within or outside

[34] Ibid., 695.
[35] *The Rites*, 759–908.
[36] Ibid., 769.
[37] Ibid., 771–74.
[38] See Parenti, "Care and Anointing," 184.
[39] *The Rites*, 778–89.

of Mass, the commendation of the dying, prayers for the dead, and rites for exceptional circumstances. These include the continuous rites of penance and anointing requested by *Sacrosanctum Concilium*, as well as rites for emergencies and for Christian initiation of the dying. A final part contains readings, responses, and verses from Sacred Scripture.

In time, supportive documentation was revised. The 1982 Code of Canon Law updated its administrative legislation concerning the anointing.[40] The *Catechism of the Catholic Church* treats the sacrament with a reflection on Christ as physician, yet one who made human misery his own. It calls healing a sign of salvation. It also surveys the history of anointing. The *Catechism* lists as effects of the sacrament the gift of the Holy Spirit, union with the passion of Christ, ecclesial grace, and preparation for one's final journey of life.[41]

The United States Conference of Catholic Bishops has issued several editions of its *Ethical and Religious Directives for Catholic Health Care Services*. Its general introduction includes another reflection on human suffering in light of the hopeful message from Jesus' life, death, and resurrection. The introduction to the first part stresses the commitment of Catholic health care to the promotion and defense of human dignity, under the biblical mandate to care for the poor.[42]

The history of anointing the sick shows how the church in every age has offered the ministry that seemed most fitting to the circumstances of human life and suffering.

Justice

The sacrament of the anointing of the sick is one way the Catholic Church aims to restore justice to the world through the physical and spiritual health of its members. This mission continues the ministry

[40] *The Code of Canon Law* (Vatican City/Washington, DC: Libreria Editrice Vaticana/Canon Law Society of America, 1983), 998–1007.

[41] *Catechism of the Catholic Church*, ed. United States Catholic Conference (Allen, TX: Thomas More, 1994), 1499–1532.

[42] *Ethical and Religious Directives for Catholic Health Care Services*, http://www.usccb.org/issues-and-action/human-life-and-dignity/health-care/upload/Ethical-Religious-Directives-Catholic-Health-Care-Services-fifth-edition-2009.pdf, accessed May 14, 2014.

of Jesus, who entrusted it to his followers. The church prays for God to undo the injustice of illness, either through its removal or through a loosening of its power over the whole person. Even when a person is dying, the church prays that the cessation of life may clear a path to a new life where peace and justice reign. Thus this sacrament applies the principles of justice to each member's hopes for physical health and eternal life.

The Second Vatican Council's revision of this rite expressed the church's desire for a broader distribution of justice. This is evident in the purpose of the anointing, the person being anointed, the occasion for the sacrament, and its minister.

The council dislodged anointing from the rites for the dying and placed it among other efforts in pastoral care. This shift has been both successful and frustrating. For the most part, Catholics understand that a priest may anoint people long before they are dying, and many attest to the power of this sacrament during their illness. However, priests may be unaware of less active sick Catholics, whose families may wait until quite late before contacting the parish. Priests may not be able to respond in a timely way, and some of those who could have been anointed never are. If families make their needs known, the prayers of the church appeal to a just and loving God when divine assistance is needed most.

As the purpose of the anointing changed from a final forgiveness before death into a prayer for better health and salvation, more persons became eligible. Many people whose conditions have weakened with advanced age are more susceptible to illnesses that can ravage a compromised system. They make good candidates for anointing and have derived comfort from it. However, some who really do not qualify still receive the sacrament. One should not judge by appearances—after all, many seriously ill people appear to be fit and strong. But others may present themselves for inappropriate reasons: an illness of no great magnitude, the emotional disquiet that accompanies the stresses of life, or the desire to stand in proxy for someone who is sick. Such persons demonstrate how easily this anointing can be misunderstood. By relaxing the requirements from those who are dying, the church made it harder for some to judge when the sacrament is appropriate. It is still an anointing "of the sick"; it does not aim to set right every possible injustice on the human person.

The revised rites have also addressed the sickness and dying of children. Nothing feels more unfair than ill health stealing happiness and hope from a child. In its compassion for those who must wrestle with these realities, the church provided for the first time in history special texts to benefit an ailing child.[43]

A person may now be anointed more than once, especially if there has been some change in condition. In practice, it is common to anoint a person more than once. Residents of nursing homes, possessors of chronic illnesses, and elderly members of a community probably receive this sacrament more than once a year, even if their condition appears stable. People often sense the time to be anointed. They may request the sacrament on their own, or they may come when it is offered. In either case, they seek the peace that ill health and advanced age can easily threaten.

The anointing may take place during Mass or whenever the community is gathered. When a family requests anointing for a member, the priest may arrange a time when several people can be present. Sometimes when a priest enters a hospital room or home to anoint, family and friends offer to leave. However, their presence demonstrates the community's care for the sick.

Priests now have permission to bless oil if they do not have access to oil blessed by the bishop, as long as they do so within the Rite of Anointing. This eliminated the potential difficulty in which a priest is available to anoint but has no blessed oil. The church seeks various ways to achieve justice for those burdened with ill health.

The Catholic Church restricts the ministry of anointing to priests and bishops. This ensures that the powerful prayers of the ordained will be summoned when other members of the church need them most. However, by restricting the sacrament to priests, anointing is less available than it was in the fifth century when Pope Innocent I acknowledged that all Christians could anoint the sick. Interestingly, the Rite calls the priest "the only proper minister,"[44] not "the only minister." This does not exclude the possibility of an extraordinary minister, and there is anecdotal evidence of bishops delegating reli-

---

[43] *Pastoral Care of the Sick: Rites of Anointing and Viaticum* (Totowa, NJ: Catholic Book Publishing Corp, 1983), 168–74.

[44] *Pastoral Care of the Sick*, 16.

gious women to be ministers of the sacrament,[45] but the Code of Canon Law as it stands today clearly restricts its administration to priests.[46]

Popular culture still uses the expression "last rites," even though it has fallen into disuse within the church. It is incorrect to say that a priest must be present for last rites. A priest must be present to anoint the sick, but any communion minister can offer viaticum, and any layperson can say prayers for the dying. A good pastor will want to attend a parishioner who is dying, but his presence is not required for the final prayers of the church, especially if he has had the opportunity earlier to anoint.

Significant to the question of justice is how the sick themselves are ministers to the church. Not every prayer for better health achieves its aim, but those who are sick contribute to the well-being of the body of Christ. Their sickness raises questions like, "Is God angry with me?" Their perseverance presents examples of faithfulness and hope. Thus even those who lack the justice of good health may achieve the justice of interior peace and minister that peace to others. Fears descend on the sick when diagnosed, but as they walk through the perils of illness, they become witnesses to the full meaning of all that God created them to be.

[45] Parenti, "Care and Anointing," 187.
[46] CCL 1003. See Parenti, "Care and Anointing," 186.

Contributors

John F. Baldovin, SJ, PhD, a Jesuit priest, is professor of historical and liturgical theology at Boston College School of Theology and Ministry in Chestnut Hill, Massachusetts.

Doris Donnelly, PhD, is professor of theology at John Carroll University and director of the Cardinal Suenens Center.

Michael S. Driscoll, STD, PhD, a priest of the Diocese of Helena, Montana, teaches sacramental theology and liturgy at the University of Notre Dame and is codirector of the Master in Sacred Music Program at the University of Notre Dame.

Edward P. Hahnenberg, PhD, holds the Jack and Mary Jane Breen Chair in Catholic Systematic Theology at John Carroll University in Cleveland, Ohio.

Thomas J. Scirghi, SJ, a Jesuit priest, is associate professor of theology at Fordham University, New York.

Paul Turner, STD, a priest of the Diocese of Kansas City–St. Joseph, Missouri, is pastor of St. Anthony Parish in Kansas City, Missouri.

Natalie Kertes Weaver, PhD, is professor and chair of the Department of Religion and director of the Humanities Program at Ursuline College in Pepper Pike, Ohio.

Made in the USA
Monee, IL
28 December 2020

55773551R20069